COMING EVENTS and PRESENT DUTIES

Register This New Book

Benefits of Registering*

- ✓ FREE **replacements** of lost or damaged books
- ✓ FREE **audiobook** – *Pilgrim's Progress*, audiobook edition
- ✓ FREE information about new titles and other **freebies**

www.anekopress.com/new-book-registration

*See our website for requirements and limitations.

COMING EVENTS and PRESENT DUTIES

WHAT THE BIBLE TELLS US CLEARLY
ABOUT CHRIST'S RETURN

J. C. RYLE

We enjoy hearing from our readers. Please contact us
at www.anekopress.com/questions-comments with
any questions, comments, or suggestions.

Coming Events and Present Duties
© 2022 by Aneko Press
All rights reserved. First edition 1867.
Revisions copyright 2022.

Please do not reproduce, store in a retrieval system, or transmit in any form
or by any means – electronic, mechanical, photocopying, recording, or
otherwise, without written permission from the publisher. Please contact us
via www.AnekoPress.com for reprint and translation permissions.

Scripture quotations from The Authorized (King James) Version. Rights in the
Authorized Version in the United Kingdom are vested in the Crown. Reproduced
by permission of the Crown's patentee, Cambridge University Press.

Cover Designer: Jonathan Lewis
Editors: Charlene Miskimen and Ruth Clark

Aneko Press
www.anekopress.com
Aneko Press, Life Sentence Publishing, and our logos are trademarks of
Life Sentence Publishing, Inc.
203 E. Birch Street
P.O. Box 652
Abbotsford, WI 54405

RELIGION / Biblical Studies / Prophecy
Paperback ISBN: 978-1-62245-839-4
eBook ISBN: 978-1-62245-840-0
10   9   8   7   6   5   4   3   2   1
Available where books are sold

Contents

Preface to Second Edition vii

Preface ix

Ch. 1: Watch 1

Ch. 2: Occupy Till I Come 31

Ch. 3: What Time Is It? 53

Ch. 4: Idolatry to Be Destroyed at Christ's Coming 73

Ch. 5: Scattered Israel to Be Gathered 93

Ch. 6: The Reading Which Is Blessed 113

Ch. 7: And So All Israel Shall Be Saved 135

Ch. 8: The Heirs of God 151

J. C. Ryle – A Brief Biography 175

Other Similar Titles 179

Preface to Second Edition

As I grow older, I can only say that I am more and more convinced that one great secret of Christian peace is to keep our eyes steadily fixed on the second coming of Christ.

If this book helps just one reader to develop the habit of looking at Christ's coming again, as well as Christ crucified and Christ interceding, I will be satisfied.

J. C. Ryle
Stradbroke Vicarage,
October 1879

Preface

The book you are now holding requires a few introductory words of explanation. It contains little that is entirely new. It consists of eight sermons preached on public occasions at different times during my ministry and afterward published in the form of tracts. Of these sermons, one or two might have been circulated more than they deserved, while one or two, which in my humble judgment are of more real worth, have received comparatively little notice. They are now compiled in their present form for the convenience of those who wish to have a condensed manual of my views of prophecy.

At the very beginning, I warn you that you will find here nothing deep or obscure. I have purposely avoided everything that can be called speculative or conjectural. I have strictly confined myself to a few great prophetic principles, which appear to me written, as it were, with a sunbeam. I have not tried to expound such portions of God's Word as Ezekiel's temple, or the symbolic visions of Revelation. I have not tried to set any dates. I have not tried to settle the precise order or manner in which predictions of things to come are to be fulfilled. There is nothing I dislike so much in prophetic inquiry as dogmatism or overconfidence. Much of the discredit that has fallen on prophetic study has arisen from the fact that many students, instead of expounding prophecy, have turned into prophets themselves.

If anyone asks me what my prophetic opinions are, I am quite ready to give an answer. As cautious and doubtful as I feel on some points, there are certain great principles about which I have fully made up my mind. I have held by them firmly for many years and have never had my opinion shaken about them. I have believed them for more than thirty years, and I expect to still believe them when I die. The older I grow, the more convinced I feel of their truth, and the more satisfied am I that no other principles can explain the state of the church and the world.

I want to explain one thing before making my statement. The reader must distinctly understand that I do not propose my prophetic views as articles of faith, but only as my personal opinions. I do not say that only those who agree with me about prophecy can be saved. I am not infallible. I am very aware that holier and better men than I do not see these subjects the same way I do and may think I am completely mistaken. I do not condemn or judge anyone. I only ask for the liberty to hold and plainly state my own views. The day will come when we will all see who is right. It is the new heart and faith in Christ's blood that are absolutely necessary to salvation. The person who knows these two things experimentally might be wrong about prophecy but will not miss heaven.

The following, then, are the main articles of my prophetic creed:

1. I believe the world will never be completely converted to Christianity by any existing agency before the end comes. Despite all that can be done by ministers, churches, schools, and missions, the wheat and the tares will grow together until the harvest, and when the end comes, the earth will be in much the same state that it was when the flood came in the days of Noah (Matthew 13:24-30; 24:37-39).

2. I believe the widespread unbelief, indifference, formalism, and wickedness seen throughout Christendom are only what we are taught in God's Word to expect. Troublesome times, departures from the faith, evil men becoming even more evil, and love growing cold are distinctly predicted. So, far from making me doubt the truth of Christianity, they instead help to confirm my faith. Melancholy and sorrowful as the sight is, if I did not see it, I would think the Bible was not true (Matthew 24:12; 1 Timothy 4:1; 2 Timothy 3:1, 4, 13).

3. I believe the grand purpose of the present age is not to convert all mankind, but to gather out of the world an elect people. It does not surprise me at all to hear that the heathen are not all converted when missionaries preach, and that believers are but a little flock in any congregation in my own land. It is precisely the state of things that I expect to find. The gospel is to be preached as a witness and then the end will come. Now is the time of election, not of universal conversion (Matthew 24:14; Acts 15:14).

4. I believe the second coming of our Lord Jesus Christ is the great event that will wind up the present age and is the event we should long for and pray for every day. *Thy kingdom come* and *Come, Lord Jesus* should be our daily prayer. If we have faith, we look backward to Christ dying on the cross, and if we have hope, we must look forward to Christ coming again (John 14:3; 2 Timothy 4:8; 2 Peter 3:12).

5. I believe the second coming of our Lord Jesus Christ will be a real, literal, personal, bodily coming, and as He went away in the clouds of heaven with His body before the eyes of men, so in the same way He will return (Acts 1:11).

6. I believe that after our Lord Jesus Christ comes again, the earth will be renewed and the curse removed; the devil will be bound, the godly will be rewarded, and the wicked will be punished. Before He comes there will be neither resurrection, judgment, nor millennium, and not until after He comes will the earth be filled with the knowledge of the glory of the Lord (Isaiah 25:6-9; Acts 3:21; 1 Thessalonians 4:14-18; Revelation 20).

7. I believe that the Jews, after going through tribulation, will ultimately be gathered again as a separate nation, restored to their own land, and converted to the faith of Christ (Jeremiah 30:10-11; 31:10; Daniel 12:1; Zechariah 13:8-9; Romans 11:25-26).

8. I believe that both in the past and now in the present, the

church has neglected the literal sense of the Old Testament prophecies, and that under the mistaken system of spiritualizing and accommodating Bible language, Christians have too often completely missed its meaning (Luke 24:25-26).

9. I do not believe that either the preterist view of interpreting Revelation, which regards the book as almost entirely fulfilled, or the futurist view, which regards it as almost entirely unfulfilled, are to be implicitly followed. The truth, I expect, will be found to lie somewhere between the two.

10. I believe the Roman Catholic Church is the great predicted apostasy from the faith and is Babylon and antichrist, although I think it highly probable that a more complete development of antichrist will yet be exhibited to the world (1 Timothy 4:1-3; 2 Thessalonians 2:3-11).

11. Finally, I believe that it is for the safety, happiness, and comfort of all true Christians to expect as little as possible from present churches or governments, to hold themselves ready for tremendous convulsions and changes of all established things, and to expect any good things only from Christ's second advent.

The student of prophecy will immediately see that there are many subjects on which I abstain from giving an opinion: the precise time when the present age will end, the manner in which unbelievers will be converted, the process by which the Jews will be restored to their own land, the burning up of the earth, the first resurrection, the rapture of the saints, the distinction between the appearing and the coming of Christ, the future siege of Jerusalem and the last tribulation of the Jews, the binding of Satan before the millennium begins, the duration of the millennium, the loosing of Satan at the end of the thousand years, the destruction of Gog and Magog, and the precise nature and place of the new Jerusalem. About all these things I purposely decline to express any opinion. I could say something about them all, but it would be little better than conjecture. I am thankful that others have more understanding than I have, but right now I feel unable to speak confidently. If I have learned anything in studying prophecy, I think I have learned the wisdom of not rushing to decide what is true.

I understand the views I have stated here appear to many to be very gloomy and discouraging. The only answer I make to that charge is to ask, "Are they scriptural? Are they in keeping with the lessons of history and experience?" To my mind they certainly are. I see human failure and human corruption stamped on the conclusion of all ages preceding our own, and I see much in the current state of the world that makes me expect these present times will not end any better. We humans seem to cause decay in everything that we touch. There is no such thing as creature perfection. There will be no perfection until the Lord comes. God is teaching that lesson by His successive ways of dealing with mankind; the patriarchal, the Mosaic, and the Christian dispensations all tend to prove it. Those words of Scripture will be verified: *I will overturn, overturn, overturn, it: and it shall be no more, until he come whose right it is; and I will give it him* (Ezekiel 21:27). When the Lord Jesus comes back to earth, and the tabernacle of God is with men, then there will be perfection, but not until then. God will have all the glory at last, and all the world will confess that without God man can do nothing. God will be *all in all* (1 Corinthians 15:28).

> God will have all the glory at last.

The one idea on which I want to focus is the second personal coming of my Lord and Savior Jesus Christ. I hope, by God's help, to point all who read this book to that *blessed hope, and the glorious appearing* (Titus 2:13). God forbid that anyone should neglect present duties! To sit idly waiting for Christ, and not to attend to the business of our respective positions is not Christianity but fanaticism. Let us only remember in all our daily pursuits that we serve a *Master who is coming again*. If I can stir up just one Christian to think more of that second coming and to give it more prominence, I feel that this book will not have been published in vain.

If anyone asks me why I have chosen this particular time for the republication of these prophetic tracts, I think it is sufficient to point to the times in which we live. I do not forget that we are poor judges of our own days and are very apt to exaggerate their importance. But I doubt whether there was ever a time in the history of our country when the horizon on all sides, both political and ecclesiastical, was so thoroughly black and lowering. In every direction we see *men's hearts failing them for fear, and for looking after those things which are coming on the earth* (Luke 21:26). Everything around us seems unscrewed, loosened, and out of joint. The fountains of the great deep appear to be breaking up. Ancient institutions are tottering and ready to fall. Social and religious systems are failing and crumbling away. Church and state both seem convulsed to their very foundations, and what the end of this convulsion may be no one can tell.

Whether the last days of old England have really come, whether her political greatness is about to pass away, whether her Protestant church's light will go out, whether in the coming crash of nations England is to perish like Amalek[1] or will suffer but eventually be saved – all these are points which I dare not attempt to settle. They will all be decided in just a short time. But I am sure there never was a time when it was more important to call believers to stop trusting in men (Isaiah 2:22), to be on guard, and to build all their hopes on the second coming of the Lord. Happy is he who has learned to expect little from parliaments or councils, from statesmen or from bishops, and to look steadily for Christ's appearing! That person will not be disappointed.

– J. C. Ryle
    Stradbroke Vicarage, August 1867

P.S. You will probably notice that some of the thoughts and ideas in this book are occasionally repeated. Kindly remember that this is because the sermons which make up this book were given in different places and with much time in between. For many reasons, I have thought it best to reprint them without alteration.

---

[1] The Amalekites were enemies of the Israelites and were condemned to annihilation (Deuteronomy 25; 1 Samuel 15).

Chapter 1

Watch

Then shall the kingdom of heaven be likened unto ten virgins, which took their lamps, and went forth to meet the bridegroom. And five of them were wise, and five were foolish. They that were foolish took their lamps, and took no oil with them: But the wise took oil in their vessels with their lamps. While the bridegroom tarried, they all slumbered and slept. And at midnight there was a cry made, Behold, the bridegroom cometh; go ye out to meet him. Then all those virgins arose, and trimmed their lamps. And the foolish said unto the wise, Give us of your oil; for our lamps are gone out. But the wise answered, saying, Not so; lest there be not enough for us and you: but go ye rather to them that sell, and buy for yourselves. And while they went to buy, the bridegroom came; and they that were ready went in with him to the marriage: and the door was shut. Afterward came also the other virgins, saying, Lord, Lord, open to us. But he answered and said, Verily I say unto you, I know you not. Watch therefore, for ye know neither the day nor the hour wherein the Son of man cometh. (Matthew 25:1-13)

The passage of Scripture before us is one that deserves the close attention of all professing Christians. We ought to read it again and again until we are thoroughly familiar with every sentence it contains.

It is a passage that concerns us all, whether ministers or laypeople, rich or poor, educated or uneducated, young or old. It is a passage that can never be known too well.

These thirteen verses make up one of the most serious parables that our Lord Christ ever spoke, partly because of the time at which it was spoken, and partly because of the matter which it contains.

As to the time, it was but a few days before our Lord's crucifixion. It was spoken within view of Gethsemane and Calvary, of the cross and the grave.

As to the matter, it stands as a sign to the church of Christ in all ages. It is a clear witness against carelessness and slothfulness, and against apathy and indifference toward religion. It cries to thoughtless sinners, "Awake!" It cries to true servants of Christ, "Watch!"

This parable opens up many trains of thought that I must ignore. I do not sit down to compose a scholarly commentary but to write a simple, practical address. I will explain two things which otherwise might not be understood. And when I have done that, I will keep to those main truths that are most useful for us to know.

The marriage customs of ancient Israel, where the parable was spoken, call for a few words of explanation. Marriages there generally took place in the evening. The bridegroom and his friends came in procession to the bride's house after nightfall. The young women who were the bride's friends were all gathered there waiting for them. As soon as the lamps and torches carried by the bridegroom's party were seen coming in the distance, these young women lighted their lamps and went out to meet them. Then, with the bridegroom's party, they all returned together to the bride's home. As soon as they arrived there, they entered in, the doors were shut, the marriage ceremony went forward, and no one else was admitted. All these were familiar things to those who heard the Lord Jesus speak, and you too should have them in your mind's eye while you read this parable.

The figures and emblems used in the parable also call for some explanation. I will give you my own view of their meaning. I may be wrong; I freely admit that they are not always interpreted exactly in the same way. But you have a right to hear my opinion, and I will give it you briefly and decisively.

I believe the parable to be a prophecy all the way through.

I believe the time spoken of in the parable is the time when Christ will return in person to this world, a time yet to come. The very first word of Matthew 25, the word *then,* compared with the end of the previous chapter, appears to me to settle that question.

I believe the ten virgins carrying lamps represent the whole body of professing Christians, the visible church of Christ.

I believe the bridegroom represents our Lord Jesus Christ Himself.

The wise virgins are the true believers, the real disciples of Christ, the converted part of the visible church.

The foolish are Christians in name only, the unconverted, the whole company of those who have no genuine godliness.

I believe the lamps are the mere outward profession of Christianity. Those who have been baptized and have not renounced their baptism possess this.

The oil, which some virgins had with their lamps and others had not, is the grace of the Holy Spirit, that anointing of the Holy One (1 John 2:20) which is the mark of all true Christians.

I consider the coming of the bridegroom to mean the second personal coming or advent of the Lord Christ, when He will return in the clouds with glory.

I consider the meaning of the wise virgins going into the marriage to be the believer's entrance into his full reward in the day of Christ's appearing.

I consider the shutting out of the foolish virgins to mean the exclusion from Christ's kingdom and glory of every person He finds unconverted at His second advent.

I offer these short explanations for your attention. I am not going to enter into any unprofitable discussion about them. And without saying another word in the way of preface, I will at once go on to point out the great practical lessons that the parable of the ten virgins teaches.

1. The visible church of Christ will always be a mixed body until Christ comes again.

2. The visible church is always in danger of neglecting the doctrine of Christ's second advent.

3. Whenever Christ does come again, it will be a very sudden event.

4. Christ's second advent will cause an immense change to all the members of the visible church, both good and bad.

Let me try to set each of these four truths plainly before you. If I can bring you, by God's help, to see their importance, I believe I will have done you a great service.

The visible church of Christ will always be a mixed body until Christ comes again.

This is the only meaning I can gather from the beginning of this parable. There I see wise and foolish virgins mingled together in one group, virgins with oil and virgins with no oil, all side by side. And this continues until the very moment the bridegroom appears. I see all this and cannot avoid the conclusion that the visible church will always be a mixed body until Jesus comes again. Its members will never be all unbelievers; Christ will always have His witnesses. Its members will never be all believers; there will always be a vast proportion of formality, unbelief, hypocrisy, and false profession.

I frankly say that I can find no basis for the common opinion that the visible church will gradually advance to a state of perfection, that it will become better and better and holier and holier up to the very end, and that little by little, the whole body will become full of light. I see no justification in Scripture for believing that sin will gradually dwindle away in the earth; that it will melt and disappear by inches, like the last snowdrift in spring. Neither do I see grounds for believing that holiness will gradually increase, like the banyan tree of the East, until it blossoms, blooms, and fills the face of the world with fruit. I know that thousands think this way. All I say is that I cannot see it in God's Word.

I fully admit that the gospel sometimes appears to make rapid progress in some countries, but I deny that it ever does more than call out an elect people. It never did more in the days of the apostles. There is not the slightest proof that in any of the cities that Paul visited the whole population became believers. That has never happened in any country from the time of the apostles down to the present day. There never has been a parish or congregation in any part of the world, no matter how blessed its ministry, in which all the people were converted. In any event, I have never read or heard of it, and my belief is that the thing never has happened and never will. I believe that now is the time of election, not of universal conversion. Now is the time for the gathering out of Christ's little flock; the time of general obedience is not yet here.

I fully admit that missions are doing a great work among the unsaved and that schools and clergy are rescuing thousands from the devil at home. I do not undervalue these things. I wish that all professing Christians would value them more. But men appear to forget that the religion of the gospel is often withering in one place while it is flourishing in another. They look at the progress of Christianity in Western Europe, but they forget how fearfully it has lost ground in the East. They point to the little flood tide of Tinnevelly and Krishnaghur.[2] They forget the tremendous ebb in North Africa, Egypt, and Asia Minor. And in the way our world is now, there are no signs that all the ends of the earth will turn to the Lord. God's work is going forward, as it always has done. The gospel is being preached for a witness in every quarter of the globe. The elect are being brought to Christ one by one, and this encourages us to persevere, but nowhere in the world can any missionary report more than this.

> Now is the time for the gathering out of Christ's little flock.

I long for the conversion of all people as much as anyone. But I believe it is utterly beyond the reach of any tool that man possesses. I quite expect that the earth will one day be filled with the knowledge of the glory of the Lord. But I believe that day will be in an entirely new dispensation; it will not be until after the Lord's return. I would not hesitate to preach the gospel and offer Christ's salvation to every man and woman alive, but I am convinced that until the second advent, there will always be a vast amount of unbelief and wickedness. The net of the gospel may perhaps be spread far more widely than it has ever been before, but in the last day, the angels will find an abundance of bad fish in it as well as good. There may be millions more people working for the gospel, and I pray that might be, but however faithfully they may

---

2   Tinnevelly and Krishnaghur were regions in India that were the home of many Christian converts in the mid-1800s.

sow, a large proportion of tares will be found growing together with the wheat at the time of harvest.

How is it with your own soul? Remember, until the Lord Jesus Christ comes again, there will always be wise and foolish ones in the church. Which are you?

The wise are those who have that wisdom which the Holy Spirit alone can give. They know their own sinfulness. They know Christ as their own precious Savior. They know how to walk and please God, and they act upon their knowledge. They look on life as a season of preparation for eternity, not as an end, but as a way; not as a harbor, but as a voyage. They see life not as a home, but as a journey; not as their adulthood, but as their childhood. Those who know these things are happy! The world may despise them, but they are the wise.

The foolish are those who are without spiritual knowledge. They do not know God, or Christ, or sin, or their own hearts, or the world, or heaven, or hell, or even the value of their own souls. There is no folly like this. To expect wages after doing no work, prosperity after making no effort, or learning after neglecting books is utter foolishness. But to expect heaven without faith in Christ, or the kingdom of God without being born again, or the crown of glory without the cross and a holy walk – all this is greater folly still and yet more common. Sadly, this is the foolishness of the world!

Until the Lord Jesus Christ comes, in the visible church there will always be some who have grace and some who do not. Now which are you? How is it with your own soul?

Some have nothing but the name of *Christian,* others have the reality. Some have only the outward profession of religion, others have the possession also. Some are content if they belong to the church, others are never content unless they are also united by faith to Christ. Some are satisfied if they have only the baptism of water, others are never satisfied unless they also feel within the baptism of the Spirit and the sprinkling of the blood of atonement. Some stop short with having the outward form of Christianity, others never rest until they also have the substance.

The visible church of Christ is made up of these two groups. It always has been and it always will be. There are those in the middle who waver and hesitate regarding faith in Christ, but these are seen only by God and are invisible to man. But the whole visible church of Christ is made up of the gracious and the graceless, the wise and the foolish. You yourself are described and written down in this parable. You are either one of the wise virgins or one of the foolish. You either have the oil of grace or you have none. You are either a member of Christ or a child of the devil. You are traveling either toward heaven or toward hell. Never for a moment forget this. This is the point that concerns your soul. Whatever your opinion may be on other points, this is the one that you should never lose sight of. Do not let the devil divert your attention from it. Say to yourself as you read this parable, "I am spoken of here."

> The visible church is always in danger of neglecting the doctrine of Christ's second advent.

The visible church is always in danger of neglecting the doctrine of Christ's second advent.

I draw this truth from that solemn verse in the parable: *While the bridegroom tarried, they all slumbered and slept.* I am quite aware that many good men explain these words in a different way. But I dare not call any man master. I need to proclaim what my own conscience tells me is true, and I cannot be bound by the opinions of others. There are such things as erroneous interpretations received by tradition, as well as false doctrines passed down to us, and we need to be on our guard against both.

I do not believe that the words *they all slumbered and slept* mean the death of all, though many think so. Such an interpretation is contrary to plain facts. All the professing church will not be sleeping the sleep of death when Jesus comes again. Paul himself says in one place, *We shall not all sleep, but we shall all be changed* (1 Corinthians 15:51), and in another, *We which are alive and remain shall be caught up . . . to meet the Lord in the air* (1 Thessalonians 4:17). So this interpretation, that all will die, involves a most awkward contradiction of these two plain texts.

Neither do I believe that the words were meant to teach us that the whole professing church will get into a slumbering and sleeping state of soul, though many think so. Many would understand this. I will not deny that the love of even the brightest Christians is very cold, and neither their faith nor their works are what they ought to be. All I mean to say is that this is not the truth which appears to me to be taught here. Such a view of the text seems to me to wipe away that broad line of distinction between believers and unbelievers, which, even with all the shortcomings of believers, undoubtedly does exist. Sleep is one of those emblems which the Spirit has chosen to represent the state of the unconverted. *Awake thou that sleepest,* He says, *and arise from the dead, and Christ shall give thee light* (Ephesians 5:14).

But what does the verse mean? I believe that the words *all slumbered and slept* are to be interpreted with a special regard to the great event on which the whole parable hinges – the second advent of Christ. And I believe our Lord's meaning was simply this: that during the interval between His first and second advent, the whole church, both believers and unbelievers, would view the blessed doctrine of His own personal return to earth with apathy and indifference.

In my own judgment, I believe there never was a saying of our Lord's more thoroughly verified by the event. Of all doctrines of the gospel, the one about which Christians have become most unlike the first Christians in their sense of its true value is the doctrine of Christ's second advent. I say this of all denominations of Protestants; I do not know of any exception. In our view of man's corruption, of justification by faith, of our need of the sanctifying work of the Spirit, of the sufficiency of Scripture – upon these points I believe that today's believers are of much the same mind with the believers in Corinth, Ephesus, Philippi, and Rome of former times. But in our view of the second advent of Christ, I fear we would find there was a great difference between us and them if our experience could be compared. I am afraid we would find that we fall woefully short of them in our estimate of its importance; that in our system of doctrine it is a very dim and far-off star, while in theirs it was one of the brightest. Compared to them in this matter, we slumber and sleep.

I must speak on this subject, but I do so unwillingly. I do so at the risk of offending many whom I love. But I feel it is my duty to speak up.

In the matter of Christ's second coming and kingdom, the church of Christ has not dealt fairly with the prophecies of the Old Testament. For too long we have refused to see that there are two personal advents of

Christ spoken of in those prophecies: an advent in humiliation and an advent in glory, an advent to suffer and an advent to reign, a personal advent to carry the cross and a personal advent to wear the crown. We have been *slow of heart to believe **all** that the prophets have spoken* (Luke 24:25 emphasis added). The apostles went to one extreme: they stumbled at Christ's sufferings. We have gone to the other: we have stumbled at Christ's glory. We have gotten into the confused habit of speaking of the kingdom of Christ as already set up here among us and have shut our eyes to the fact that the devil is still prince of this world and is served by the vast majority, and that our Lord, though like David in Adullam, has been anointed but not yet set upon His throne (1 Samuel 22). We have a vicious habit of taking all the promises spiritually and all the denunciations and threats literally. We have been content to take the condemnations against Babylon, Nineveh, Edom, Tyre, Egypt, and the rebellious Jews literally and hand them over to our neighbors. The blessings and promises of glory to Zion, Jerusalem, Jacob, and Israel we have taken spiritually and comfortably applied them to ourselves and the church of Christ. To bring forward proofs of this would be a waste of time. You do not need to listen to many sermons or read many commentaries to be aware that it is a fact.

This is an unfair system of interpreting Scripture. I hold that the first and primary sense of every Old Testament promise, as well as each threat, is the literal one, and that Jacob means Jacob, Jerusalem means Jerusalem, Zion means Zion, and Israel means Israel, as much as Egypt means Egypt, and Babylon means Babylon. We have lost sight of that primary sense. We have adapted and applied to the church of Christ the promises that were spoken by God to Israel and Zion. I do not mean to say that this accommodation is never allowable. But I do mean to say that the primary sense of every prophecy and promise in Old Testament prophecy was intended to have a literal fulfillment and that this literal fulfillment has been put aside and thrust into a corner. And by so doing I think we have exactly fulfilled our Lord's words in the parable of the ten virgins: we have proved that we are slumbering and sleeping about the second advent of Christ.

But I also believe that in the interpretation of the New Testament, the church of Christ has dealt almost as unfairly with our Lord's second advent as she has done in the interpretation of the Old Testament. We have made a habit of putting a strange sense upon many of those passages which speak of the coming of the Son of Man or of the Lord's appearing. And we have submitted too easily to it. Some tell us that the coming of the Son of Man often means death. No one can read the thousands of epitaphs in churchyards in which some text about the coming of Christ is thrust in, and not perceive how widespread this view is. Some tell us that our Lord's coming means the destruction of Jerusalem. This is a very common way of interpreting the expression. Many find the literal Jerusalem everywhere in New Testament prophecies, though, oddly enough, they refuse to see it in the Old Testament prophecies, and, like Aaron's rod, they make it swallow up every other interpretation. Some tell us that our Lord's coming means the general judgment and the end of all things. This is their one answer to all questions about things to come.

Now I believe that all these interpretations entirely miss the mark. I do not have any desire to underrate the importance of subjects such as death and judgment. I willingly concede that the destruction of Jerusalem is one of many things connected with our Lord's second advent and is spoken of in chapters where that mighty event is foretold. But my own firm belief is that the coming of Christ is one distinct thing, and that death, judgment, and the destruction of Jerusalem are three other distinct things. And the wide acceptance which these strange interpretations have gained is one more proof that in the matter of Christ's second advent, the church has long slumbered and slept.

The plain truth of Scripture is this: when the number of the elect is accomplished, Christ will come again to this world with power and great glory. He will raise His saints and gather them to Himself. He will punish severely all who are found to be His enemies, and will gloriously reward all His believing people. He will take to Himself His great power, and will reign and establish a universal kingdom. He will gather the scattered tribes of Israel and place them once more in their own land. As He came the first time in person, so He will come the second time in person. As He went away from earth visibly, so He will return visibly. As He literally rode upon a donkey, was literally sold for thirty pieces of silver, had His hands and feet literally pierced, was numbered literally with the transgressors, and had lots literally cast for His garments – all so that Scripture might be fulfilled – so also He will literally come, literally set up a kingdom, and literally reign over the earth because the very same Scripture has said it will be so.

The words of the angels in the first chapter of Acts are plain and unmistakable: *This same Jesus, which is taken up from you into heaven, shall so come in like manner as ye have seen him go into heaven* (Acts 1:11). Similar words are spoken by the apostle Peter: *The times of refreshing shall come from the presence of the Lord. And he shall send Jesus Christ, which before was preached unto you: whom the heaven must receive until the times of restitution of all things, which God hath spoken by the mouth of all his holy prophets since the world began* (Acts 3:19-21). And again, by the psalmist and Zechariah and Isaiah and Jeremiah and Daniel: *When the Lord shall build up Zion, he shall appear in his glory* (Psalm 102:16); *The Lord my God shall come, and all the saints with thee* (Zechariah 14:5); *The Lord of hosts shall reign in mount Zion, and in Jerusalem, and before his ancients gloriously* (Isaiah 24:23); *I will bring again the captivity of my people Israel and Judah, saith the Lord: and I will cause them to return to the land that I gave to their fathers, and they shall possess it* (Jeremiah 30:3); *I will bring again the captivity of Jacob's tents, and have mercy on his dwellingplaces; and the city shall be builded upon her own heap* (Jeremiah 30:18); *Behold, one like the Son of man came with the clouds of heaven, and came to the Ancient of days, and they brought him near before him. And there was given him dominion, and glory, and a kingdom, that all people, nations, and languages, should serve him: his dominion is an everlasting dominion, which shall not pass away, and his kingdom that which shall not be destroyed* (Daniel 7:13-14). All these texts are plain prophecies of Christ's second coming and kingdom. They have yet to be accomplished, but all will be literally and exactly fulfilled.

I say "literally and exactly fulfilled" after great consideration. From the first day that I began to read the Bible with my heart, I have never been able to see these texts and hundreds like them in any other light. It always seemed to me that as we take literally the texts foretelling that the walls of Babylon will be cast down, so we ought to take literally the texts foretelling that the walls of Zion will be built up. If according to prophecy the Jews were literally scattered, so according to prophecy the Jews will be literally gathered. And that as the least and minutest predictions were made good on the subject of our Lord's coming to suffer, so the minutest predictions will be made good which describe our Lord's coming to reign. One of the greatest shortcomings of the church of Christ is that we ministers do not preach enough about this advent of Christ and that laypeople do not think enough about it. A few of us here and there profess to love the doctrine, but the number of such persons is relatively small. And none of us live on it, feed on it, act on it, work from it, or take comfort in it as much as God intended us to. In short, the Bridegroom tarries and we all slumber and sleep.

This doctrine of Christ's second coming and kingdom is not any less true just because it has sometimes been abused. All doctrines of the gospel have been misused and misapplied. Salvation by grace has been made a pretext for licentiousness, election an excuse for all manner of unclean living, and justification by faith a warrant for antinomianism.[3] But we are not obliged to throw away good principles because men draw the wrong conclusions from them. We do not give up the gospel because of the outrageous conduct of the Anabaptists of Munster,[4] or the extravagant assertions of Saltmarsh and William Huntingdon,[5] or the strange proceedings of Jumpers and Shakers.[6] And it is not fair to tell us that we ought to reject the second advent of Christ because there were Fifth Monarchy Men in the days of the Commonwealth and Irvingites and Millerites[7] in our own time. Men must be hard-pressed for an argument when they have no better reasons than these!

Those who hold the doctrine of the second coming of Christ differ

---

[3] *Antinomianism,* a term coined by Martin Luther, means "anti-law" and is often used to describe the belief that Christians do not need to obey the law of God; they can live however they choose.

[4] This refers to a group of Anabaptist revolutionaries with strong apocalyptic views who controlled the city of Munster by violent force, mandated baptism, and encouraged polygamy.

[5] John Saltmarsh and William Huntingdon were religious leaders who were accused of teaching antinomianism.

[6] The Jumpers and Shakers were the followers of Mary Ann Girling, a religious leader in England in the 1870s. Girling was known for her excited jumping while preaching and promoting her views on celibacy and communal life.

[7] Fifth Monarchy Men was an extreme religious group that taught that Christ was coming back within months and was going to come to England. The Irvingites and Millerites were sects that focused heavily on the imminent second advent, promising the return of the apostolic gifts (Irvingites) and a set date for the return of Christ (Millerites).

among themselves on many points of prophecy, but that does nothing to diminish the doctrine. Those who remember that unity on great points is perfectly consistent with disagreement on small ones will not stumble. Luther and Zwingli differed widely in their views of the Lord's Supper, yet who would think of saying that therefore Protestantism is all false? Fletcher and Toplady were both clergymen in the Church of England, but differed widely about Calvinism; but what would be the sense of saying that all evangelical religion was therefore untrue? To be fair, people ought to remember this when they talk of the differences among those who study prophecy. It is possible to greatly disagree on the meaning of the symbols in the book of Revelation, yet agree entirely and substantially on the matter of Christ's coming and kingdom.

I concede that the doctrine contains many difficulties, but that proves nothing against it. The order of events connected with our Lord's coming and the manner of His kingdom when it is set up are both deep subjects and hard to understand. But I believe there are twice as many difficulties connected with any other system of interpreting unfulfilled prophecy. I also believe that there are twice as many difficulties connected with our Lord's first coming as those connected with His second, and that it was a far more improbable thing. It is *a priori,* more reasonable, that the Son of God should come to suffer, than it is that He should come to reign. And after all, it does not concern us as to "how" and "in what manner" prophecies are to be fulfilled. Is our miserable understanding of what is possible to be the measure and limit of God's actions? The only question for us is, "Has God said it?" If He has, then we should not doubt it will be done.

I can only give my own individual testimony, but the little I know experimentally of the doctrine of Christ's second coming convinces me to regard it as most practical and precious, and makes me long to see others regard it the same way.

I find it a powerful spring and stimulus to holy living, a motive for patience, for moderation, for spiritual-mindedness, a test for how I use my time, and a gauge for all my actions. "Would I want my Lord to find me in this place, doing what I am doing?"

I also find it to be the strongest argument for missionary work. The time is short. The Lord is at hand. The gathering out from all nations will soon be accomplished. The heralds and forerunners of the King will soon have proclaimed the gospel in every nation. The night is almost gone. The King will soon be here.

It is the best answer to the infidel. He sneers at our churches and chapels, at our sermons and services, at our tracts and our schools. He points to the millions who still care nothing for Christianity even after eighteen hundred years of preaching. He asks me how I can account for this if Christianity is true. I answer that it was never said that all the world would believe and serve Christ under the present dispensation. I tell him that the things he ridicules were predicted, and the number of true Christians was expected to be few. But I tell him that Christ's kingdom has not yet come, and even though we still have not seen all things put under Him, one day we will.

I find it to be the best reasoning to use with a Jew. If I do not take all the prophecy of Isaiah literally, I do not know how I can persuade him that the fifty-third chapter is fulfilled literally. But if I do, I have an argument which I know he cannot shake. How men can expect Jews to see in Old Testament prophecies a Messiah coming to suffer if they do not themselves see in them a Messiah coming to reign is past my understanding.

And now, is there any one of you who cannot accept the doctrine of Christ's second advent and kingdom? I invite you to consider the subject calmly and impartially. Dismiss from your mind traditional interpretations. Separate the doctrine from the mistakes and blunders of many who hold it. Do not reject the foundation because of the wood, hay, and stubble which some have built upon it. Do not condemn it and cast it aside because of misguided friends. Examine the texts which speak of it as calmly and fairly as you weigh texts in other controversies, and I am hopeful of the result. If texts of Scripture were always treated as unceremoniously as I have known texts to be treated by those who dislike the doctrine of Christ's second advent, I would tremble for the cause of truth!

Is there any one of you who agrees with the principles I have tried to advocate? I beg you to make real the second coming of Christ more and more. We feel it but very little compared to what we ought to. Be gentle in argument with those that differ from you. Remember that a man may be mistaken on this subject, but yet be a holy child of God. It is not the slumbering on this subject that ruins souls, but the lack of grace! Above all, avoid dogmatism and overconfidence, especially when dealing with symbolic prophecy. It is a sad truth, but a truth never to be forgotten, that none have injured the doctrine of the second coming more than its overzealous friends.

Whenever Christ does come again, it will be a very sudden event.

This truth comes from the verse in the parable that says, *At midnight there was a cry made, Behold, the bridegroom cometh; go ye out to meet him.*

I do not know when Christ will come again. It would be presumptuous if I said that I did. I am no prophet, though I love the subject of prophecy. I dislike setting dates and naming years, and I believe it has done great harm. I only state confidently that Christ will one day come again to set up His kingdom on earth, and that whether the day be near or whether it be far, it will take the church and the world by exceeding surprise.

It will come on men suddenly. It will break on the world all at once. It will not have been talked over, prepared for, and looked forward to by everyone. It will awaken minds like the cry of fire at midnight. It will startle hearts like a trumpet blown at bedside during a dead sleep. Like Pharaoh and his host in the Red Sea, they will know nothing until the very waters are upon them. Like Dathan, Abiram, and their followers when the earth opened under them, the moment they hear the report of Christ's coming will be the same moment they see it with their eyes (Numbers 16). Before they can recover their breath and know where they are, they will find that the Lord has come.

> **It will be a very sudden event.**

I suspect there is a vague notion floating in our minds that the present order of things will not end quite so suddenly. I suspect some cling to the idea that there will be a kind of Saturday night in the world, a time when all will know the day of the Lord is near; that there will be a time when all will be able to cleanse their consciences, look for and find their wedding garments, shake off their earthly business, and prepare to meet their God. If anyone has this thought, I command you to give it up forever. If anything is clear in unfulfilled prophecy, this one fact seems clear: the Lord's coming will be sudden and will take men by surprise. Any view of prophecy which destroys the possibility of its being sudden, either by introducing many events that still need to take place or by placing the millennium between ourselves and the advent – any such view appears to me to carry a fatal defect. Everything that is written in Scripture on this point confirms the truth that Christ's second coming will be sudden. *As a snare shall it come,* says one place (Luke 21:35). *As a thief in the night,* says another (1 Thessalonians 5:2). A third says it will come *as the lightning* (Luke 17:24), and a fourth and fifth tell us when: *in such an hour as ye think not* (Matthew 24:44), and *when they shall say, Peace and safety* (1 Thessalonians 5:3).

Our Lord Jesus Christ Himself uses two most striking comparisons when speaking on this subject. Both are instructive and ought to raise in us serious thoughts. In the first, He compares His coming to the days of Lot. When Lot fled from Sodom, the men of Sodom were buying and selling, eating and drinking, planting and building. They thought of nothing but earthly things; they were entirely absorbed in them and despised Lot's warning. They mocked his advice. The sun rose on the earth as usual. Things were going on as they had for hundreds of years. They saw no sign of danger. But notice what our Lord says: *The same day that Lot went out of Sodom it rained fire and brimstone from heaven, and destroyed them all. Even thus shall it be in the day when the Son of man is revealed* (Luke 17:29-30).

In the other passage I refer to, our Lord compares His coming to the days of Noah. Do you remember how it was in Noah's day? Let me remind you. Before the flood came on the earth in Noah's time, there was no visible sign of anything so awful being near. The days and nights were following each other in regular succession. The grass, and trees, and crops were growing as usual. The business of the world was going on. And though Noah preached continually of coming danger and warned men to repent, no one believed what he said. But at last, one day the rain began and did not cease, the waters rose and did not stop, the flood came and swelled and went on and covered one thing after another. All were drowned who were not in the ark. Listen to what our Lord says: *As it was in the days of Noe, so shall it be also in the days of the Son of man. They did eat, they drank, they married wives, they were given in marriage, until the day that Noah entered into the ark, and the flood came, and destroyed them all* (Luke 17:26-27). The flood took the world by surprise, and so will the coming of the Son of Man. In the middle of the world's business when things are going on as usual is when the Lord Jesus Christ will return.

The suddenness of the Lord's second advent is a truth that should prompt all Christians to search their hearts. It should lead them to seriously think about both themselves and the world.

Think for a moment how little the world is prepared for such an event. Look at the towns and cities of the earth and notice how most people are entirely absorbed in the things of this life and consumed with their careers. Banks, shops, politics, law, medicine, commerce, transportation, banquets, balls, theaters – each and all are consuming the hearts and souls of thousands and thrusting out the things of God. Think what a fearful shock will come in the day of Christ's appearing with the sudden stoppage of all these things. If just one corporation declares bankruptcy now, it makes a great sensation. What then will be the crash when the whole machine of worldly affairs stands still at once? From counting money and making plans, from racing after riches and arguing about trifles, to be hurried away to meet the King of Kings – how tremendous the change! To go from dancing and dressing, from going to concerts and reading novels, to being summoned away by *the voice of the archangel, and with the trump of God* – how awful the transition! Remember, one day all this will be.

Think about the rural parishes in such a land as ours. Look how most of their residents are immersed in farms and allotments, in cattle and corn, in rent and wages, in rates and tithes, in digging and sowing, in buying and selling, in planting and building. See how many there are who evidently care for nothing and feel nothing except the things of this world, who do not pay any attention to whether their minister preaches law or gospel, Christ or antichrist, and who would be utterly unconcerned if the archbishop of Canterbury were turned out of Lambeth Palace and the pope of Rome put in his place. See how many there are of whom it can only be said that their bellies and their pockets are their gods. And then imagine the awful effect of a sudden call to meet the Lord Christ, a call to a day of reckoning in which the price of wheat and the rate of wages will be nothing, and the Bible will be the only rule of trial! And remember, one day all this will be.

Picture these things: your house, your family, your fireside. What will be found there? Picture above all your own feelings, your own state of mind. And then remember that this is the end towards which the world is rushing. There will be no warning far in advance. This is the way in which the world's affairs will be brought to an end. This is an event which may happen in your own time, and you cannot conclude that the second coming of Christ is mere curious speculation. It is an event of enormous practical importance.

But I can imagine someone saying, "This is all foolishness and raving nonsense. This writer is a fanatic; he's out of his mind. What is the likelihood, the probability of all this? The world is going on as it always did. It's not going to end in my lifetime." Do not say this. Do not ignore the subject by talking like this. This is the way men talked in the days of Noah and Lot, but what happened? They found to their loss that Noah and Lot were right. Do not say so. The apostle Peter foretold eighteen hundred years ago that men would talk this way. *There shall come in the last day scoffers,* he tells us, *saying, Where is the promise of his coming? for since the fathers fell asleep, all things continue as they were from the beginning of the creation* (2 Peter 3:3-4). Oh, do not fulfill his prophecy by your unbelief!

> I calmly assert that the present order of things will come to an end one day.

Where is the madness and fanaticism of the things which I have been saying? Show it to me if you can. I calmly assert that the present order of things will come to an end one day. Will anyone deny that? Will anyone tell me we will go on forever as we do now? I calmly say that Christ's second coming will be the end of our normal way of life. I have said so because the Bible says it. I have calmly said that Christ's second coming will be a sudden event, whenever it may be, and may possibly be in our own time. I have said so, because that is the way I find it written in the Word of God. If you do not like it, I am sorry. You must remember one thing: you are finding fault with the Bible, not with me.

Christ's second coming will cause an immense change to all members of the visible church, both good and bad.

I draw this truth from the concluding portion of the parable – from the discovery of the foolish virgins that their lamps had gone out, from their anxious plea to the wise: *Give us of your oil;* from their vain knocking at the door when too late, crying, *Lord, Lord, open to us;* from the happy admission of the wise who were found ready in company with the bridegroom. These points are full of food for thought, but I have neither time nor space to dwell upon each one particularly. I can only take a broad view. To all who have been baptized in the name of Christ, converted or unconverted, believers or unbelievers, holy or unholy, godly or ungodly, wise or foolish, gracious or graceless – to all – the second advent of Christ will be an immense change.

To the ungodly, to those who are Christian in name only, it will be an immense change to both their opinions and position.

When Christ comes again, all of these people will see the value of real spiritual religion if they never saw it before. They will do in effect what the parable illustrates: they will cry to the godly, *Give us of your oil; for our lamps are gone out.*

We all know that in the present world spiritual religion never brings the world's praise. It never has in the past and it never does now. It brings instead the world's disapproval, the world's persecution, the world's mockery, the world's opposition, the world's ridicule, the world's sneers. The world will let a man serve the devil and quietly go to hell; no one lifts a finger to stop him or even says, "May God have mercy on your soul." But the world will never let a man serve Christ and go to heaven quietly. Everybody cries, "Stop, wait!" and does anything and everything to keep him back.

Those who follow Christ and try to be saved are often belittled with nicknames – Pietists, Puritans, Methodists, Fanatics, Enthusiasts, Calvinists, Ultra-religionists, the Saints, the Righteous Overmuch, the Very Good People, and many more. We know the petty family persecutions that often go on in private society in our day. Let young people go to every party and social event but utterly neglect their souls, and no one interferes. No one says, "Save yourselves." No one says, "Be careful. Remember God, judgment, and eternity." But let them start to read their Bibles and be diligent in prayer, let them avoid worldly amusements and use their time wisely, let them seek an evangelical ministry and live like an immortal being – let them do this, I say, and all their friends and relatives will be up in arms. "You are going too far. You are being extreme. Live a little." This in all probability is the very least that such people will hear. If a young woman, she will be labeled and avoided by all her peers. If a young man, he will be marked by all who know him as weak, silly, and rigid. In short, such people will soon discover that there is no help from the world on the way to heaven, but plenty of help on the way to hell.

I wish it were not so, but it is! These are ancient things. As it was in the days of Cain and Abel, as it was in the days of Isaac and Ishmael, so it is now. *He that was born after the flesh persecuted him that was born after the Spirit, even so it is now* (Galatians 4:29). The cross of Christ will always bring reproach with it. As the Jews hated Christ, so the world hates Christians. As the Head was bruised, so also will be the members. As contempt was poured on the Master, so it will be poured on the disciples. In short, if you desire to become a decided evangelical Christian, you must "count the cost" and make up your mind to lose the world's favor. In a word, you must be content to be thought by many as little better than a fool.

There will be an end of all this when Christ returns to this world. The light of that day will at last show everything in its true colors. The scales will fall from the eyes of those who have been blinded by the pleasures of this world. The value of the soul will flash on their astonished minds. The utter uselessness of a mere nominal Christianity will burst upon them like a thunderstorm. The blessedness of regeneration, faith in Christ, and a holy walk will shine before them like MENE, MENE, TEKEL, PERES on the wall of the Babylonian palace. The veils will fall from their faces. They will discover that it has been the godly that have been the wise, and that they have played the fool. And just as Saul wanted Samuel when it was too late, and Belshazzar sent for Daniel when the kingdom was about to be taken from him, so will the ungodly turn to the very men they once mocked and despised and cry to them, *Give us of your oil; for our lamps are gone out.*

But as there will be a complete change in the opinions of the ungodly in the day of Christ's second advent, so there will also be a complete change in their position. Vain hope, the plank to which they now cling and on which they depend to the very end, will be entirely taken away in that awful day. They will seek salvation with earnestness but will not be able to find it. They will run here and there in a vain search for the oil of grace. They will knock loudly at the door of mercy and get no answer. They will cry, *Lord, Lord, open to us,* but it will be of no use. They will discover to their sorrow that opportunities once passed can never be regained, and that the notion of universal mercy is a mere delusion of the devil.

Thousands are urged to pray and repent now, but they never attempt it. They mean to – one day, perhaps. Like Felix, they hope for a convenient time (Acts 24:25). They imagine it will never be too late to seek the Lord. But there is a time coming when prayer will be heard no longer and repentance will be ineffective. There is a time when the door by which Manasseh[8] and Saul the persecutor entered will be shut and opened no more. There is a time when the fountain in which Mary Magdalene, John Newton, and thousands of others were washed and made clean will be sealed forever. There is a time when men will know the folly of sin, but like Judas, it will be too late for repentance; when they will desire to enter the promised land, but like Israel at Kadesh (Numbers 14), they will not be able to; when they will see the value of God's favor and covenant blessing, but like Esau, they can no longer possess it; when they will believe every jot and tittle of God's revealed Word, but like the miserable devils, they will only tremble.

Yes, many will come to this in the day of Christ's appearing. They will ask and not receive! They will seek and not find. They will knock and the door will not be opened to them. Sadly, this is how it will be. Woe to those who put off seeking manna until the Lord's day of return. Like Israel of old, they will find none. Woe to those who go to buy oil when they ought to be burning it! Like the foolish virgins, they will find themselves shut out from the marriage supper of the Lamb. Oh, professing Christians, consider these things! Remember that the words

---

8   Manasseh, one of the most wicked kings of Judah, sought God and repented after being taken captive to Babylon.

of our Lord have yet to be fulfilled: *When once the master of the house is risen up, and hath shut to the door, and ye begin to stand without, and to knock at the door, saying, Lord, Lord, open unto us; and he shall answer and say unto you, I know you not whence ye are: then shall ye begin to say, We have eaten and drunk in thy presence, and thou hast taught in our streets. But he shall say, I tell you, I know you not whence ye are; depart from me, all ye workers of iniquity* (Luke 13:25-27).

But as Christ's second coming will be a mighty change to the ungodly, so it will also be a mighty change to the godly. They will at last be freed from everything which now spoils their comfort. The door will be shut –against the fiery darts of Satan, against the hated weakness of the flesh which now clings to them, against the unkind world which now misrepresents and misunderstands them, against the doubts and fears which now so often darken their path, against the weariness which now obstructs their best efforts to serve the Lord, against coldness and deadness, against shortcomings and backsliding – against all these the door will be shut forever. Not one single Canaanite will be found in the land. They will no longer be frustrated by temptation, persecuted by the world, warred against by the devil. Their conflict will be over. Their strife with the flesh will cease forever. The armor of God, which they have worn so long, will at last be laid aside. They will be where there is no Satan, no sorrow, and no sin. Oh! The second Eden will be far better than the first! In the first Eden the door was not shut; our joy was just for a moment. But blessed be God, in the second Eden the Lord will shut us in.

And as the godly will enjoy freedom from all evil in the day of Christ's appearing, so they will also enjoy the presence of all good. They will go in with the Bridegroom to the marriage. They will be forever in the company of Christ and go out no more. Faith will then be swallowed up in sight. Hope will become certainty. Knowledge will at last be perfect. Prayer will be turned into praise. Desires will be attained. Hunger and thirst after conformity to Christ's image will be satisfied. The thought of parting will not spoil the pleasure of meeting. The company of fellow saints will be enjoyed without hurry and distraction. The family of Abraham will no longer feel temptations, and the family of Job will not feel afflictions. The family of David will no longer mourn loss and death, the family of Paul will not feel thorns in the flesh, and the family of Lazarus will no longer be afflicted by poverty and sores. Every tear will be wiped away in that day. It is the time when the Lord will say, *I make all things new.*

Oh, if God's children find joy and peace in believing now, how will their tongues express their feelings when they see the King in His beauty? If the report of the far-off land has been sweet to them here in the wilderness, what pen will describe their happiness when they see it with their own eyes? If it has cheered them now and then to meet two or three like-minded people in this evil world, how their hearts will burn within them when they see a multitude of true believers so large that it cannot be counted, each washed clean of all sin and defects! If the narrow way has been pleasant to the scattered few who have traveled it with their weak and frail bodies, how precious will their rest seem in the day when they are gathered together with glorious bodies like their Lord's! Then we will understand the meaning of the text: *In thy presence is fulness of joy; at thy right hand there are pleasures for evermore* (Psalm 16:11). Then we will experience the truth of that beautiful hymn that says,

> Let me be with Thee where Thou art,
>   My Saviour, my eternal rest!
> Then only will this longing heart
>   Be fully and for ever blest.
>
> Let me be with Thee where Thou art,
>   Thy unveiled glory to behold;
> Then only will this wandering heart
>   Cease to be faithless, treacherous, cold.
>
> Let me be with Thee where Thou art,
>   Where none can die, where none remove;
> Where life nor death my soul can part
>   From Thy blest presence and Thy love.[9]

---

9   This is from the hymn "Let Me Be with Thee" by Charlotte Elliott (1789–1871).

Do any of you ever laugh at true religion? Do you persecute and ridicule godliness in others, or dare to talk of people being too particular and too righteous? Beware of what you are doing! Be careful! You may live to think very differently. You may live to alter your opinion, but it will perhaps be too late. There is a day coming when there will be no unbelievers. Not one! There is a day when the disciples of Paine and Voltaire and Emerson will call on the rocks to fall on them and on the hills to cover them. Before the throne of Jesus every knee will bow and every tongue confess that He is the Lord. Remember that day and beware.

Are any of you dear children of God who are mocked and despised for the sake of the gospel and feel as if you stand alone? Take comfort. Be patient. Wait a little longer. Your turn will come. When the spies returned from searching out Canaan, men talked of stoning Caleb and Joshua because they brought a good report of the land. But after a few days, all the assembly confessed that they alone had been right. Strive to be like them. Follow the Lord fully as they did, and sooner or later all men will confess that you did well. Never, never be afraid of going too far. Never, never be afraid of being too holy. Never, never be ashamed of desiring to go to heaven and seeking to have a great crown. Millions will lament in the day of Christ's return that they do not have enough religion; not one will be heard to say that he has too much. Take comfort. Press on.

And now I will close with three words of application that seem to naturally arise out of this parable. I wholeheartedly pray that God will make these words timely and bless them to your soul.

My first word of application is a **question.** I take the parable of the ten virgins as my authorization, and I address that question to every one of you. I ask, "Are you ready?" Remember the words of the Lord Jesus: *They that were ready went in with [the bridegroom] to the marriage* – they that were ready and no one else. Here, in the sight of God, I ask you, "Are you ready?"

I do not ask if you go to church or profess to be religious. I do not ask if you attend an evangelical ministry, like evangelical people, can talk of evangelical subjects, and read evangelical tracts and books. All this is just the surface of Christianity. This costs little and may be easily attained. I want to search your heart more thoroughly and probe your conscience more deeply. I want to know if you have been born again and if you have the Holy Spirit dwelling in your soul. I want to know if you have brought extra oil while you carry the lamp of profession and if you are ready to meet the Bridegroom, ready for Christ's return to the earth. I want to know if the Lord should come this week, could you lift up your head with joy and say, *This is our God; we have waited for him, . . . we will be glad and rejoice in his salvation.* These things I want to know, and this is what I mean when I say, "Are you ready?"

But I can imagine some saying, "This is asking far too much – to be ready for Christ's appearing! This is far too high a standard. This is extravagance. It would be impossible to live in the world at this rate. This is a hard saying. Who can listen to this?" I cannot help it. I believe this is the standard of the Bible. I believe this is the standard Paul sets before us when he says the Thessalonians were *wait[ing] for [God's] Son from heaven,* and the Corinthians were *waiting for the coming of our Lord Jesus Christ* (1 Thessalonians 1:10; 1 Corinthians 1:7). And surely this is the standard Peter sets before us when he speaks of *looking for and hasting unto the coming of the day of God* (2 Peter 3:12). I believe it is a mark that every true believer should be continually aiming at – to live so as to always be ready to meet Christ. God forbid that I should place the standard of Christian practice a hair's width higher than the level at which the Bible places it. But God forbid that I should ever put it even a hair's width lower. If I do, what right do I have to say that the Bible is my rule of faith?

> I want to search your heart more thoroughly and probe your conscience more deeply.

I do not want to disqualify anyone for usefulness here on earth; you do not need to become a hermit and stop serving your generation. I do not ask you to leave your job or career and neglect your earthly affairs. But I do call on everyone to live like one who expects Christ to return; to live soberly, righteously, and godly in this present world. I ask you to live like pilgrims and strangers, ever looking to Jesus, to live like good servants, prepared for action and with your lamp burning, to live like one whose treasure is in heaven, with your heart packed up and ready to leave. This is readiness. This is preparation. Is this too much to ask? I say unhesitatingly that it is not.

Are you ready in this way? If not, I want to know what good your religion does you. What is it all but a pointless burden, a show? What is it but a mere temporary cloak that will not be worn beyond this world? Truly a religion that does not make you ready for everything – for death, for judgment, for the second advent, for the resurrection – should be looked on with suspicion. If your religion does not make you ready for anything, the sooner it is changed the better.

My second word of application will be an **invitation.** I address it to all who feel in their conscience that they have no grace in their hearts – to all who feel that the character of the foolish virgins is their own. To every such person I invite you this day, in my Master's name, to awake and flee to Christ.

If this is how you feel, you know that all that is within you is wrong in the sight of God. Nothing is truer about you than that you are asleep, not merely about the doctrine of Christ's second advent, but also about everything that concerns your soul. You are wide awake, perhaps, about worldly things. You keep up with current events and read the news. You have your head stored with earthly wisdom and useful knowledge. But you have no heartfelt sense of sin, no peace or friendship with God, no fellowship with Christ, no delight in the Bible and prayer. And you are a sinner, a dying sinner, an immortal sinner, a sinner going to meet Christ, a sinner going to be judged. Honestly, what is this but being asleep?

How long will this go on? When do you plan to arise and live as if you had a soul? When will you cease to hear as one who hears not? When will you give up running after shadows and seek something substantial? When will you throw off the mockery of a religion which cannot satisfy, cannot comfort, cannot sanctify, cannot save, and will not stand up to examination? When will you give up having a faith which does not influence your practice, having a book which you say is God's Word but treating it as if it were not, having the name of Christian but knowing nothing of Christ? Oh! When will it end?

Why not this very year? Why not this very day? Why not at once awake and call upon your God and resolve that you will sleep no longer?

I set before you an open door. I set before you Jesus Christ the Savior who died to make atonement for sinners, Jesus who is able to save to the uttermost, Jesus who is willing to receive. The hand that was nailed to the cross is held out to you in mercy. The eye that wept over Jerusalem is looking on you with pity. The voice that has said to many wanderers, *Your sins are forgiven,* is saying to you, *Come to me.* If you want to know what steps to take, go to Jesus first. Do not wait for repentance and faith and a new heart, but go to Him just as you are. Go to Him in prayer and cry, "Lord, save me, or I will die. I am tired of sleeping; I do not want to sleep any longer." Awake, you sleeper, and Christ will give you light.

The sun, moon, and stars all witness against you; they continue according to God's ordinances, but you are always violating God's laws. The grass, the birds, the very worms of the earth are all witnessing against you; they fill their place in creation, but you do not. The Sabbath and the law are continually witnessing against you; they proclaim there is a God and a judgment, but you live as if there were none. The tears and prayers of godly relatives are witnessing against you; others are sorrowfully thinking you have a soul, though you seem to forget it. The very gravestones that you see every week are witnessing against you; they are silently witnessing that life is uncertain, time is short, the resurrection is yet to come, and the Lord is at hand. All are saying, "Awake, awake, awake!" You have slept long enough. Awake to be wise. Awake to be safe. Awake to be happy. Awake and sleep no more.

My last word of application will be an **exhortation** to all true believers, to all who have grace in their hearts and have been pardoned by the blood of the Lamb. I take it from the words of the Lord Jesus at the end of the parable. I exhort you earnestly to watch.

I encourage you to watch against everything which might interfere with a readiness for Christ's appearing. Search your own hearts. Find out the things which most frequently interrupt your communion with Christ. Recognize and mark these things, and always be on your guard against them.

Watch against sin of every kind. Do not think, "Ah! I would never do that." There is no sin too abominable for the very best of us to commit. Remember David and Uriah (2 Samuel 11). The spirit may be sometimes very willing, but the flesh is always very weak. You are still in the body. Watch and pray.

If you are a believer in Christ Jesus, watch against doubts and unbelief regarding your salvation. The Lord Jesus finished the work He came to do; do not tell Him that He did not. The Lord Jesus paid your debts in full; do not tell Him that you think He left you some to pay. The Lord Jesus promises eternal life to every sinner that comes to Him; do not tell Him as you are coming that you think He lies. Oh, our unbelief! In Christ you are like Noah in the ark and Lot in Zoar – nothing can harm you. The earth may be burned up with fire at the Lord's appearing, but not a hair of your head will be harmed. Do not doubt. Pray for more faith. Watch and pray.

Watch against an inconsistent walk and conformity to the world. Watch against sins of your temper and your tongue. These are the kinds of things that grieve the Spirit of God and make His witness within us muted and weak. Watch and pray.

Watch against false doctrine. Remember that Satan can transform himself into an angel of light. Counterfeit money is never marked counterfeit or else it would never be passed. Guard jealously the whole truth as it is in Jesus. Do not put up with a grain of error for the sake of a pound of truth. Do not tolerate a little false doctrine one bit more than you would tolerate a little sin. Oh, remember this caution! Watch and pray. Watch against apathy toward the Bible and prayer. There is nothing so spiritual that it cannot be turned into just a form, an outward show. Most backsliding begins privately. When a tree is snapped in two by a high wind, we usually find there has been some long-hidden decay. Oh, watch and pray!

Watch against bitterness and unkindness toward others. A little love is more valuable than many gifts. Look for the good in others with eyes like an eagle's, but see their evil with the weak eyes of a mole. Let your memory be a safe for their virtues, but a sieve for their faults. Watch and pray.

Watch against vanity and pride. Peter insisted that even if he had to die with Jesus, he would never deny Him. And he soon fell. Pride is the high road to a fall. Watch and pray.

Watch against the sins of Galatia, Ephesus, and Laodicea. Believers may run well for a while but then lose their first love and become lukewarm. Watch and pray.

Watch against the sin of Jehu. Jehu may have appeared to have great zeal in his quest for vengeance, but yet he did not turn from the sins of Jeroboam (2 Kings 9-10). It is much easier to oppose antichrist than to follow Christ. It is one thing to protest against error; it is quite another thing to love the truth. So watch and pray.

> Let us watch that we may not be startled when the Lord appears.

Oh, let us all watch more than we have previously! Let us watch more every year that we live. Let us watch that we may not be startled when the Lord appears.

Let us watch for the world's sake. For the most part, we are the books they read. They notice our ways far more than we think. Let us aim to be clearly written and understood letters of Christ.

Let us watch for our own sakes. As our walk is consistent and pure, so will be our peace. As we conform to Christ's mind, so will our sense of Christ's atoning blood grow. If a man will not walk in the full light of the sun, how can he expect to be warm?

Above all, let us watch for our Lord Jesus Christ's sake. Let us live as if His glory were affected by our behavior. Let us live as if every slip and fall was a reflection on the honor of our King. Let us live as if every sin we allowed was one more thorn in His head, one more nail in His feet, one more spear in His side. Let us make use of a godly jealousy over thoughts, words, and actions – over motives, manners, and walk. Never fear being too strict. Never let us think we can watch too much. Few believers were more useful in their day and generation than Legh Richmond.[10] His dying words were very solemn; of him it can be truly said that even though he is dead, he still speaks (Hebrews 11:4). What did he say while he lay dying? "Brother, brother, we are none of us more than half awake!"

---

10 Legh Richmond (1772–1827) was an English pastor and the author of several books that influenced the conversion of many people.

Chapter 2

Occupy Till I Come

And as they heard these things, he added and spake a parable, because he was nigh to Jerusalem, and because they thought that the kingdom of God should immediately appear. He said therefore, A certain nobleman went into a far country to receive for himself a kingdom, and to return. And he called his ten servants, and delivered them ten pounds, and said unto them, Occupy till I come. (Luke 19:11-13)

These words form an introduction to the parable commonly called the parable of the pounds, and they contain subjects which deserve the prayerful consideration of every true Christian today.

There are some parables of which Matthew Henry says with equal quaintness and truth, "The key hangs beside the door." The "key" to understanding the parable is easily found. The Holy Spirit Himself interprets. There is no room left for doubt as to the purpose for which they were spoken. The parable of the pounds is one of these.

Luke tells us that our Lord Jesus Christ *added and spake a parable, because he was nigh to Jerusalem, and because they thought that the kingdom of God should immediately appear.* These words reveal the secret thoughts of our Lord's disciples at this period of His ministry. They were approaching Jerusalem. They gathered from what Jesus had been saying that something remarkable was about to happen. They had a strong impression that one great purpose of His coming into the world was about to be completed. So far, they were right, but as to the precise nature of the event about to happen, they were quite wrong.

There are three subjects revealed in this passage of Scripture that appear to be of great importance. I am only going to address the beginning of the parable, but for your meditation I want to direct your attention to the three following points:

1. I will speak of the mistake of the disciples referred to in this passage.

2. I will speak of the present position of the Lord Jesus Christ.

3. I will speak of the present duty of all who profess to be Jesus Christ's disciples.

I pray that God blesses all you who read this and that you will know to pray for the Spirit to guide you into truth.

What was the mistake the disciples made?

Let us try to clearly understand what this mistake was and how today's Christians should feel about this mistake. Our Lord's disciples seem to have thought that the Old Testament promises of Messiah's visible kingdom and glory were about to be immediately fulfilled. They believed rightly that he was indeed the Messiah, the Christ of God. But they blindly supposed that He was going at once to take to Himself His great power and to reign gloriously over the earth. This was the essence of their error.

They appear to have concluded that now was the day and now the hour when the Redeemer would build up Zion and appear in His glory (Psalm 102:16); when He would strike the earth with the rod of His mouth and slay the wicked with the breath of His lips (Isaiah 11:4); when He would assemble the outcasts of Israel and gather the dispersed of Judah (Isaiah 11:12); when He would take the heathen for His inheritance and the uttermost parts of the earth for His possession, break His enemies with a rod of iron and dash them in pieces like a potter's vessel (Psalm 2:8-9); when He would reign in Mount Zion, in Jerusalem, and before His ancients gloriously (Isaiah 24:23); and when the kingdom and dominion and the greatness of the kingdom under the whole heaven would be given to the saints of the Most High (Daniel 7:27). This appears to have been the mistake into which our Lord's disciples had fallen at the time when He spoke the parable of the pounds.

Unquestionably, it was a great mistake. They did not realize that before all these prophecies could be fulfilled, it was necessary for Christ to suffer (Luke 24:46); He first had to die. Their optimistic expectations leaped over the crucifixion and the long parenthesis of time to follow, and bounded on to the final glory. They did not see that there was to be a first advent of Messiah to *be cut off* (Daniel 9:26) before the second coming of Messiah to reign. They did not perceive that the sacrifices and ceremonies of the law of Moses would first be fulfilled in a better sacrifice and a better High Priest, and the shedding of blood more precious than that of bulls and goats. They did not comprehend that before the glory, Christ must be crucified and an elect people gathered out from among the gentiles by the preaching of the gospel. All these things were dark to them. They grasped part of the prophetic word but not all. They saw that Christ was to have a kingdom, but they did not see that He was to be wounded and bruised and made an offering for sin. They understood the end of the second psalm and all of the ninety-seventh and ninety-eighth, but not the beginning of the twenty-second. They understood the eleventh chapter of Isaiah, but not the fifty-third. They understood the dispensation of the crown and the glory, but not the dispensation of the cross and the shame. This was their mistake.

The disciples cling partly to this mistake even after the crucifixion. You see it in the first days of the church in the time between the resurrection and the ascension. They said, *Lord, wilt thou at this time restore again the kingdom to Israel?*[11] (Acts 1:6). You find it referred to by Paul: *Be not soon shaken in mind, or be troubled, neither by spirit, nor by word, nor by letter as from us, as that the day of Christ is at hand. Let no man deceive you by any means: for that day shall not come, except there come a falling away first* (2 Thessalonians 2:2-3). In both these instances you

---

11 "Christ did never absolutely deny His having such a visible glorious kingdom upon earth as that which His disciples looked for; only He corrected their error as to the time of this kingdom appearing. Christ did not say to them that there never should be any such restoration of the kingdom to Israel as their thoughts were running upon; only He telleth them the times and seasons were not for them to know; thereby acknowledging that such a kingdom should indeed be, as they did from the holy prophets expect. Herein was their error – not in expecting a glorious appearance of the kingdom of God, but in that they made account that this would be immediately." – *The Mysteries of Israel's Salvation* by Dr. Increase Mather, 1669.

see the same tendency to misunderstand God's purposes – to overlook the dispensation of the crucifixion and to concentrate all thought on the dispensation of the kingdom. In both, you see the same tendency to neglect the duties of the present order of things. Those duties are to bear the cross of Christ, to take part in the afflictions of the gospel, to work, to witness, to preach, and to help make disciples.

We gentile believers, however, ought to regard this mistake with kindness and careful thought. We should not consider our Jewish brothers carnal and earthly-minded because of their interpretation of prophecy as if we gentiles had never made any mistakes at all. I think we have made great mistakes, and it is time to confess it.

I believe we have made an error parallel with that of our Jewish brothers, an error less fatal in its consequences than theirs, but an error far more inexcusable because we have had more light. If the Jews thought too exclusively of Christ reigning, have not the gentiles thought too exclusively of Christ suffering? If the Jews could see nothing in Old Testament prophecy but Christ's exaltation and final power, have not the gentiles often seen nothing but Christ's humiliation and the preaching of the gospel? If the Jews spent too much time on Christ's second advent, have not the gentiles spent time almost exclusively on the first? If the Jews ignored the cross, have not the gentiles ignored the crown? I believe there is only one answer to these questions. I believe that up until lately we gentiles have been wrong about a large part of God's truth. We have clung to an arbitrary and reckless habit of interpreting first-advent texts literally and second-advent texts spiritually. I believe we have not rightly understood *all that the prophets have spoken* about the second personal advent of Christ any more than the Jews did about the first. And because we have done this, we should speak of the mistakes of the disciples with tenderness and compassion.

Give special attention to this point. I do not know what your opinions are about the fulfillment of the prophetic parts of Scripture, but I approach the subject with fear and trembling because I do not want to hurt the feelings of any fellow believers. But I ask you, in love, to examine your own views about prophecy. I urge you to calmly consider whether your opinions about Christ's second advent and kingdom are as sound and scriptural as those of His first disciples. Think carefully and pay attention so that you do not commit the same error about Christ's second coming and glory as they did about His first coming and the cross.

I beg you not to dismiss this subject as a curious theory of no real importance. Believe me, it affects the whole conversation between yourself and a Jew you may be trying to win to Christ. Unless you interpret the prophetic portion of the Old Testament simply and literally, you will find it difficult to carry on an argument with an unconverted Jew.

You would probably tell a Jewish person that Jesus of Nazareth was the Messiah promised in the Old Testament Scriptures, and you would refer to those Scriptures for proof. You would show him Psalm 22, Isaiah 53, Daniel 9:26, Micah 5:2, Zechariah 9:9, and Zechariah 11:13. You would tell him that in Jesus of Nazareth those Scriptures were literally fulfilled. You would urge him to believe these Scriptures and receive Christ as the Messiah. All this is very good; so far you would do well.

But suppose he asks if you interpret *all* the prophecies of the Old Testament with a simple, literal meaning. Suppose he asks if you believe the Messiah will literally and personally return to reign over the earth in glory, Judah and Israel will be literally restored to Palestine, and Zion and Jerusalem will be literally rebuilt and restored. When he asks these questions, what answers will you give?

Will you dare to tell him that Old Testament prophecies of this kind are not to be taken plainly and literally? Will you dare to tell him that the words *Zion, Jerusalem, Jacob, Judah, Ephraim,* and *Israel* do not mean what they seem to mean, but instead mean the church of Christ? Will you dare to tell him that the glorious kingdom and future blessedness of Zion, so often mentioned in prophecy, mean nothing more than the gradual Christianizing of the world by missionaries and the preaching of the gospel? Will you dare to tell him that you think it is worldly and unspiritual to take those Scriptures literally, worldly to expect a literal rebuilding of Jerusalem, worldly to expect a literal coming of Messiah to reign, worldly to look for a literal gathering and restoration of Israel? Oh, if you are thinking this way, be careful! Think about what you are doing!

You are putting a weapon in the hand of the unbelieving Jew, a weapon he will most likely use with irresistible power. Do you not see that you are pulling the rug out from under your own feet and supplying the Jew with a strong argument for not believing your own interpretation of Scripture? If you tell a Jewish person that it is carnal to expect the Messiah will come literally to reign, then he will reply that it is carnal to tell him that the Messiah has come literally to suffer. Do you not see that he will tell you that it is far more unspiritual for you to believe that Messiah could come into the world as a despised, crucified Man of Sorrows than it is for him to believe that He will come into the world as a glorious King? That is undoubtedly what he will say, and you will have no answer.

You must take these things seriously. Throw aside all prejudice and view this subject with calm and logical thought. I beg you to reread these prophetic Scriptures and to pray that you will not err in interpreting their meaning. Read them in the light of those two great, guiding stars, the first and second advents of Jesus Christ. Associate the rejection of the Jews, the calling of the gentiles, the preaching of the gospel as a witness to the world, and the gracious gathering out of the elect with the first advent. Connect the second advent with the restoration of the Jews, the pouring out of judgments on unbelievers, the conversion of the world, and the establishment of Christ's kingdom upon earth. Do this and you will perhaps see a meaning and fullness in prophecy that you have not seen before.

I am painfully aware that many good people do not see the subject of unfulfilled prophecy the same way that I do, and that I seem presumptuous in differing from them. But I dare not refuse anything which appears to me plainly written in Scripture. Even the best people are not infallible. I think we should remember that we must reject Protestant traditions which are not in agreement with the Bible as much as the traditions of the Church of Rome.

I believe it is past time for the church of Christ to awake out of its sleep about Old Testament prophecy. From the time of the old church fathers Jerome and Origen down to the present day, men have made a harmful habit of "spiritualizing" the words of the prophets until their true meaning has been nearly buried. It is time to lay aside traditional methods of interpretation and to give up our blind obedience to the opinions of such writers as Poole, Henry, Scott, and Clarke[12] about unfulfilled prophecy. It is time to fall back on the principle that Scripture generally means what it seems to mean, and to beware of that argument that questions ordinary beliefs, that says, "That interpretation cannot be correct, because it seems to be unspiritual!"

It is time for Christians to interpret unfulfilled prophecy by the light of prophecies already fulfilled. The curses on the Jews happened literally – so also will the blessings. The scattering was literal – so also will be the gathering. The pulling down of Zion was literal – so also will be the building up. The rejection of Israel was literal – so also will be the restoration.

We need to interpret the events that will accompany Christ's second advent by the light of those accompanying His first advent. The first advent was literal, visible, personal – so also will be His second. His first advent was with a literal body – so also will be His second. At His first advent the smallest details of the predictions were fulfilled to the very letter – so also will they be at His second. The shame was literal and visible – so also will be the glory.

It is also time to stop explaining Old Testament prophecies in a way not justified by the New Testament. What right have we to say that the words *Judah, Zion, Israel,* and *Jerusalem* ever mean anything but literal Judah, literal Zion, literal Israel, and literal Jerusalem? What precedent will we find in the New Testament? Hardly any, if any at all. In his book, *Prophetical Landmarks,* Horatius Bonar admirably writes, "There are really only two or three places in the whole New Testament – Gospels, Epistles, and Revelation – where such names are used decidedly in what may be called a spiritual or figurative state. The word 'Jerusalem' occurs eighty times, and all of them unquestionably literal, save when the opposite is expressly pointed out by the epithets 'heavenly,' or 'new,' or 'holy.' 'Jew' occurs a hundred times, and only four are even ambiguous, as Romans 2:28. 'Israel' and 'Israelite' occur forty times, and all literal. 'Judah' and 'Judea' above twenty times, and all literal."[13]

It is inadequate to argue that it is impossible to carry out the principle

---

12   Matthew Poole, Matthew Henry, Thomas Scott, and Adam Clarke were all leading commentators on the whole Bible.
13   Horatius Bonar, *Prophetical Landmarks* (London: J. Nesbit & Co., 1847).

of a literal interpretation because Christ was not a literal "door" or a literal "branch," nor was the bread in the sacrament His literal "body." When I speak of literal interpretation, I am not denying the use of figurative language. I fully admit that emblems, figures, and symbols are used in foretelling Messiah's glory, as well as in foretelling Messiah's sufferings. I do not believe that Jesus was a literal "root out of dry ground" or a literal "lamb" (Isaiah 53). What I do maintain is that prophecies about Christ's coming and kingdom foretell literal facts as truly as the prophecy about Christ being *numbered with the transgressors* (Isaiah 53:12). Prophecies about the Jews being gathered will be as literally fulfilled as those about the Jews being scattered.

Neither is it valid to argue that the principle of literal interpretation deprives the church of the use and benefit of many parts of the Old Testament; I deny the justice of that charge altogether. All things written in the Prophets concerning the salvation of individual souls may be used by gentiles as freely as by Jews. The hearts of Jews and gentiles are naturally the same. There is but one way to heaven. Both Jews and gentiles need justification, regeneration, and sanctification. Whatever is written about these subjects is just as much the property of the gentile as the Jew. Furthermore, I believe Israel as a people is a picture of the whole body of believers in Christ. Believers now may take comfort in every promise of pardon, comfort, and grace that is addressed to Israel. All believers share these in common. All I insist on is that whenever God says He will do or give certain things to Israel and Jerusalem in this world, we ought to entirely believe that to literal Israel and Jerusalem those things will be given and done.

It is not a valid argument to say that many who think as I do about prophecy have said and written very foolish things and have often contradicted one another. This may be true, but the principles for which we contend are scriptural, sound, and correct. The unbeliever does not overturn the truth of Christianity when he points to the existence of antinomians, Jumpers, and Shakers. The worldly man does not overturn the truth of real evangelical religion when he sneers at the differences of Calvinists and Arminians. One writer on prophecy may interpret

Revelation or Daniel in one way, and another writer in another way. One man may set dates and then be proven wrong, and another may apply prophecies to living individuals and be utterly mistaken. But all these things do not affect the main issue. They do not in the least prove that the premillennial advent of Christ is not a scriptural truth or that the principle of interpreting Old Testament prophecy literally is not a sound principle.

I say once more that we ought to regard the mistakes of our Lord's disciples with great tenderness and consideration. We Christians should be the last to condemn them strongly; great as their mistakes were, our own have been almost as bad. We have been very quick to discover the beam in our Jewish brother's eyes and have forgotten the large speck in our own. By our arbitrary and inconsistent explanations of Old Testament prophecy, we have for a long time been putting a great stumbling block in his way. Let us do our part to remove that great obstacle. If we want to help remove the veil that prevents the Jews from seeing the cross, we need to also strip off the veil from our own eyes and look steadily and unflinchingly at the second advent and the crown.[14]

What is the present position of our Lord Jesus Christ?

The parable distinctly answers this question in the twelfth verse. *A certain nobleman went into a far country to receive for himself a kingdom, and to return.* This nobleman represents the Lord Jesus Christ in two respects.

Like the nobleman, the Lord Jesus has gone into a far country to receive for Himself a kingdom. He has not yet received it in possession, though He has in promise. Unquestionably, He has a spiritual kingdom. He is King over the hearts of His believing people, and they are all His faithful subjects. Without controversy, He has controlling power over the world. He is King of Kings and Lord of Lords. *By him all things consist,* and nothing can happen without His permission. But His real, literal, visible, and complete kingdom He has not yet received. To use the words of Hebrews 2:8, *We see not yet all things put under him;* and

---

14 For further reading see Horatius Bonar's *Prophetical Landmarks,* Andrew Bonar's *Redemption Drawing Nigh,* George Ogilvy's *Popular Objections to the Premillennial Advent Considered,* Hugh M'Neile's *Sermons on the Second Advent* and *Prospects of the Jews,* and Edward Bickersteth's *A Practical Guide to the Prophecies.*

of Psalm 110:1, *The LORD said unto my Lord, Sit thou at my right hand, until I make thine enemies thy footstool.*

The devil is *the prince of this world* during the present age (John 14:30). The majority of earth's inhabitants choose the things that please the devil far more than the things that please God. Though they may not think it, they are doing the devil's will, behaving as the devil's subjects, and serving the devil far more than Christ. This is the condition of Christian nations as well as non-Christian countries. After eighteen hundred years of Bibles and gospel preaching, there is not a nation, a country, a parish, or a long-established congregation where the devil has not more subjects than Christ. The world is not yet the kingdom of Christ.

The Lord Jesus during the present dispensation is like David between the time of his anointing and Saul's death: He has the promise of the kingdom, but has not yet received the crown and the throne (1 Samuel 22:1-2). He is followed by a few, often neither great nor wise, but they are faithful people. He is persecuted by His enemies and often driven into the wilderness, and yet His party is never completely destroyed. But He has none of the visible signs of the kingdom now – no earthly glory, majesty, greatness, or obedience. Most of mankind see no beauty in Him. They do not want this Man to reign over them. His people are not given honor because of their Master; they walk the earth like princes in disguise. His kingdom has not yet come. His will is not yet done on earth, except by a few. It is not the day of His power. The Lord Jesus is biding His time.

Grasp this truth firmly, for there are many delusions about the subject of Christ's kingdom. Be careful you are not deceived by teaching based on tradition alone. Hymns are composed and sung which darken God's teaching on this subject by using words incorrectly. Texts are wrested from their true meaning and applied to the present, texts which are not rightly applicable to any period except the period of the second advent. Watch for the subtle ways in which this is done. Beware beautiful poetry whose language sneakily twists unfulfilled promises of glory and adapts them to the present dispensation. Get it straight in your mind that Christ's kingdom is still to come. His arrows are not yet sharp in the hearts of His enemies. The day of His power has not yet begun. He is gathering out a people to carry the cross and walk in His steps. But the time of His coronation has not yet arrived.

But just as the Lord Jesus, like the nobleman, *went . . . to receive for himself a kingdom,* so like the nobleman, the Lord Jesus intends one day *to return.* The words of the angels (Acts 1:11) will be completely fulfilled: *This same Jesus, which is taken up from you into heaven, shall so come in like manner as ye have seen him go into heaven.* As His going away was a real, literal going away, so His return will be a real, literal return. As He came personally the first time with a body, so He will come personally the second time with a body. As He came visibly to this earth and visibly went away, so when He comes the second time, He will visibly return. And then, and not until then, the complete kingdom of Christ will begin. He left His servants as a nobleman; He returns to His servants as a king.

Then He intends to cast out that old usurper the devil, to bind him for a thousand years, and to strip him of his power (Revelation 20:1-3).

Then He intends to restore all of creation (Acts 3:21). It will be the world's jubilee day. Our earth will at last produce her harvest. The King will at last reign over all the earth. The ninety-seventh psalm will finally be fulfilled, and men will say, *The Lord reigneth; let the earth rejoice.*

Then He intends to fulfill the prophecies of Enoch, John the Baptist, and Paul, *to execute judgment upon all* the ungodly inhabitants of Christendom, to *burn up the chaff with unquenchable fire,* and *in flaming fire taking vengeance on them that know not God, and that obey not the gospel* (Jude v. 15; Matthew 3:12; 2 Thessalonians 1:8).

Then He intends to raise His dead saints and gather His living ones, to gather together the scattered tribes of Israel, and to set up an empire on earth in which every knee will bow to Him and every tongue confess that He is the Lord.

How, when, where, and in what manner all these things will be we cannot say with certainty. It is enough for us to know that they will be. The Lord Jesus has committed to doing them, and they will be done. The Lord Jesus waits for the time appointed by the Father, and then He will make all come to pass. As certainly as He was born of a pure virgin and lived thirty-three years on earth as a servant, so just as certainly He will come with clouds in glory and reign on the earth as a king.

Add to the established truths of your religion that Christ is one day to have a complete kingdom in this world; His kingdom is not yet set up, but it will be set up in the day of His return. Know clearly whose kingdom it is now; it is not Christ's, but the usurper Satan's. Know clearly who will one day rule this kingdom: not Satan who has been ruling without right, but Jesus Christ. Know clearly that this change of power will occur when the Lord Jesus returns in person and not before. Know clearly what the Lord Jesus is doing now: He is sitting at the right hand of the Father, interceding as a High Priest in the holy of holies for His people, adding to their number those who are being saved by the preaching of the gospel, and waiting until the appointed day of His power (Psalm 110:3) when He will come to bless His people and sit as *a priest upon his throne* (Zechariah 6:13). Know these things clearly, and you will do well.

If you do know and understand these things, then you will not expect too much from any church, minister, or religious organization in this present age. You will not wonder why ministers and missionaries are not converting all to whom they preach. You will not be surprised to find that while some believe the gospel, many do not. You will not be depressed when you see so many children of the world and so few children of God. You will remember that *the days are evil* (Ephesians 5:16) and that the time of universal conversion has not yet arrived. You will thank God that any are converted at all, and that while the gospel is hidden to the wise and prudent, it is revealed to babes. Pity the person who expects a millennium before the Lord Jesus returns! How can this possibly be if the world in the day of His coming is as it was in the days of Noah and Lot (Luke 17:26-30)?

Know these things clearly and you will not be confounded or surprised by the continuation of immense evil in the world. Wars, tumults, oppression, dishonesty, selfishness, covetousness, superstition, bad government, and abounding heresies will not appear to you inexplicable. You will not sink down into an unhealthy, cynical state of mind when you see laws, reforms, and education not making mankind perfect. You will not relapse into a state of apathy and disgust when you see churches full of imperfections and theologians making mistakes. You will say to yourself, "The time of Christ's power has not yet come; the devil is still working among his children and sowing darkness and division among the saints. The true King is yet to come."

Know these things clearly and then you will see why God delays the final glory and allows things to go on as they do in this world. It is not that He is not able to prevent evil – He is not slack in fulfilling His promises – but the Lord is taking out for Himself a people by the preaching of the gospel (Acts 15:14). He is long-suffering to the unconverted. *The Lord is . . . not willing that any should perish, but that all should come to repentance* (2 Peter 3:9). Once the number of the elect is gathered out of the world, once the last elect sinner is brought to repentance – then the kingdom of Christ will be set up and the throne of grace will be exchanged for the throne of glory.

> The Lord is taking out for Himself a people by the preaching of the gospel.

If you know these things clearly, you will work diligently to do good to people. The time is short. *The night is far spent, the day is at hand* (Romans 13:12). The "signs of the times" call loudly and certainly for watchfulness. The Turkish empire is fading. The Jews are cared for as they have never been before. The gospel is being preached as a witness in almost every corner of the world. If we want to save a few more people from destruction, we must work hard and lose no time. We must preach, we must warn, we must exhort, we must give money, we must spend and be spent far more than we have ever done.

Know these things clearly and you will then often look for the coming of the day of God. You will center all your hopes on the glorious and comfortable truth of the second advent. You will not merely think of Christ crucified, but you will also think of Christ coming again. You will long for the days of refreshing and the manifestation of the sons of God, when the glory of Christ is revealed in them (Acts 3:19; Romans 8:19). You will find peace in looking back to the cross, and you will find joyful hope in looking forward to the kingdom.

I repeat, clearly know Christ's present position. He is like one who *went into a far country to receive for himself a kingdom, and [then] to return.*

What is the present duty of all Christ's professing disciples?

When I say "present duty," I mean, of course, their duty between the period of Christ's first and second advents. And I find the answer in the words of the nobleman to his servants: He *delivered them ten pounds, and said unto them, Occupy till I come.*

There are few words more convicting and impressive than these four: *Occupy till I come.* They are spoken to all who profess and call themselves Christians. They address the conscience of those who have not renounced their baptism and formally turned their back on Christianity. They ought to provoke all who hear the gospel to examine themselves and prove whether they are in the faith. Bear with me while I try to explain why these words, which were written for your sake, are so important.

The Lord Jesus tells you to occupy. By that He means that you are to be a *doer* of your Christianity and not merely a hearer and professor of faith. He wants His servants to receive His wages, eat His bread, live in His house, and belong to His family, but He also wants them to do His work. You are to *let your light so shine before men, that they may see your good works* (Matthew 5:16). Do you have faith? It must not be a dead faith; it must work *by love* (Galatians 5:6). Are you elect? You are elect to *obedience* (1 Peter 1:2). Are you redeemed? You are redeemed so you may be *a peculiar people, zealous of good works* (Titus 2:14). Do you love Christ? Prove your love to be real by keeping Christ's commandments (John 14:15). Do not forget this charge to occupy! Beware of an idle, talking, gossiping, sentimental, do-nothing religion. Do not think that because your actions cannot justify you or erase one single sin, it does not matter whether you do anything at all. Get rid of such a delusion! Throw it behind you as an invention of the devil. Think of the house built upon the sand and its miserable end (Matthew 7:26-27). To *make your calling and election sure,* be a doing Christian.

But the Lord Jesus also commands you to occupy your talent. By this He means that He has given each one of His people some opportunity to glorify Him. He wants you to understand that everyone, the poorest and the richest, has his own sphere, has an open door before him and may, if he chooses, display his Master's praise. Your bodily health and strength, your mental gifts and capacities, your money and your earthly possessions, your rank and position in life, your example and influence with others, your liberty to read the Bible and hear the gospel, and all the many ways grace is shown to you – all these are your "talents." All these you are to use and employ, continually giving the glory to Christ. All these are His gifts. Riches and honor come from Him (1 Chronicles 29:12). The silver and the gold belong to Him (Haggai 2:8). Your body and your spirit are His (1 Corinthians 6:20). He determines where you live and He gives you life and breath (Acts 17:25-26). You are not your own. You were bought at a price (1 Corinthians 6:20). Certainly, it is just a small matter that He tells you to honor Him and serve Him with all that you have. Is there any man or woman who has not received anything from the Lord? Not one, I am sure. Make sure you set aside your money for the Lord's work consistently and honestly. Use well what He gives you; take care not to bury your talent!

But the Lord Jesus bids you also to occupy till He comes. By that He means that you are to do His work on earth like one who continually looks for His return. You are to be like the faithful servant who does not know when his master is coming home but keeps all things in order and is always prepared. You are to be like one who knows that Christ's coming is the great accounting day and to be ready to submit your account at any moment. You are not to suppose that you own anything in this world, not even a lease. The greatest and the richest of mankind is only renting with God's permission month to month. You are not to neglect any social duties or relationships because of the uncertainty of the Lord's return. You are to fill the role to which God has called you in a godly and Christian way, and you are to be ready, if the Lord chooses, to go straight from your place of business or daily activities to meet Christ in the air. You are to be like a person who never knows what a day might bring, and so you do not put things off until a "better time." You are to get up and be ready in the morning, if need be, to meet Christ at noon. You are to lie down in bed at night ready, if need be, to be awakened by the midnight cry, *Behold, the bridegroom cometh*! You are to keep your spiritual accounts in a state of constant preparation, like one who never knows how soon they may be called for. You are to make all your decisions in light of Christ's appearing and do nothing that you would not like Jesus to find you doing. This is to occupy until Jesus comes.

Think how condemning these words are to thousands of professing Christians! What a complete absence of preparation appears in their daily walk and conversation! How thoroughly unfit they are to meet Christ! They know nothing of occupying or exercising the gifts of God as loans for which they must give account. They show not the slightest desire to glorify Him with body and spirit, which are His (1 Corinthians 6:20). They show no sign of being ready for the second advent. "Well," says old Gurnall,[15] "it may be written on the grave of every unconverted man, 'Here lies one who never did for God an hour's work.'" It is not surprising that in a world like this a minister often cries to his congregation, *Ye must be born again. Except ye be converted, and become as little children, ye shall not enter into the kingdom of heaven* (John 3:7; Matthew 18:3).

Think again how inspiring these words ought to be to all who are rich in this world, but do not know the right way to spend their money. Regrettably, there are many who live their lives as if Christ had never said anything about the difficulty of rich men being saved. They spend their money for their own pleasures, their own tastes, and their own families, but not for God! They live as if they will not have to give an account of how they spent their money. They live as if there were no judgment day in the courtroom of Christ. They live as if Christ had never said, *It is more blessed to give than to receive* (Acts 20:35). *Sell that ye have, and give alms; provide yourselves bags which wax not old, a treasure in the heavens that faileth not* (Luke 12:33). Oh! If you are living this way, I beg you to consider what you are doing and be wise. Stop being content to give God's cause a few dollars. Give far more liberally than you have done before. Give hundreds where you now give tens. Give thousands where you now give hundreds. Then, and not until then, I will believe you are occupying, as one who looks for Christ's return. Oh, how sad the covetousness and narrow-mindedness of the church in these days! May the Lord open the eyes of rich Christians.

Think how instructive these words are to all who are troubled by doubts about mingling with the world and taking part in its diversions.

---

15 William Gurnall was an English author and clergyman during the seventeenth century.

It is useless to tell us that many of the world's amusements are not forbidden by name in Scripture. The question we should ask ourselves is simply this: "Am I using my time as one who looks for Christ's return when I take part in these things? Would I be ashamed to have my Lord find me there?" This is the true test by which to try all our daily activities and use of time! That thing which we would not do if we thought Jesus was coming tonight, we should not do at all. That place to which we would not go if we thought Jesus was coming this day, that place we should avoid. That company in which we would not like Jesus to find us, with those people we should never sit down. Oh, live your lives as if Christ is watching – not men, or ministers, or the church – but Christ! This would be occupying till He comes.

> Sin will no longer be made light of and disguised.

But think how encouraging these words are to all who seek first the kingdom of God and who sincerely love the Lord Christ – even though the children of the world regard them as excessively holy, even though friends and family tell them they go too far with their religion. Those words, *Occupy till I come,* are words which justify their conduct. They can reply to their persecutors, "I am doing a great work, and I cannot come down; I am striving to live so as to be ready when the Lord comes; *I must be about my Father's business.*"

Let me conclude by making some application. First, there is a *solemn warning* for everyone who reads this. That warning is that there is a great change still to come on this world and one we ought to keep constantly in view.

That change is a change of masters. That old rebel, the devil, and all his followers will be thrown down. The Lord Jesus and all His saints will be exalted and raised to honor. *The kingdoms of this world [will] become the kingdoms of our Lord, and of His Christ* (Revelation 11:15).

That change is a change of manners. Sin will no longer be made light of and disguised. Wickedness will no longer go unrebuked and unpunished. Holiness will become the general character of the inhabitants of the earth. The *new heavens and a new earth [will be] wherein dwelleth righteousness* (2 Peter 3:13).

That change is a change of opinion. There will be no more confusion about the deity, the nature, and the identity of Christ. All nations will honor the crucified Lamb of God. All men, from the least to the greatest, will know Him. *The earth shall be full of the knowledge of the LORD, as the waters cover the sea* (Isaiah 11:9).

I will say nothing about the time when these things will take place because I object, on principle, to all dogmatism about dates. What I insist on is that there is a great change coming – a change for the earth, a change for man, and above all, a change for the saints.

I accept the prediction that there will be in the future "a great improvement and development of human nature." I believe it with all my heart. But how and when will it be brought about? Not by any system of education! Not by any political legislation! Not by anything short of the appearing of the kingdom of Christ. Then, and only then, will there be universal justice, universal knowledge, and universal peace.

I accept the common phrase, "There is a good time coming." I believe it with all my heart. I do believe there will one day be no more poverty, no more oppression, no more ignorance, no more grinding competition, no more covetousness. But when will that good time come? Never! Not until the return of Jesus Christ. And for whom will that good time be? For those who know and love the Lord.

I accept the common phrase, "There is a man coming who will set all right that is now wrong. We wait for the coming man." I believe it with all my heart. I do look for One who will unravel the tangled skein of this world's affairs and put everything in its right place. But who is the Great Physician for an old, diseased, and worn-out world? It is *the man Christ Jesus,* who is yet to return.

Oh, understand this! There is a great change coming for us all, and without question, when you have been served notice that you need to leave your current home, you need to make sure you have another one to go to. Let me summarize this whole subject with a question, an invitation, and an exhortation. The question is simply this: Are you ready for the great change? Are you ready for the coming and kingdom of Christ? I am not asking what you think about controversial points of prophecy nor your opinion about the timing of events. I am not asking if you think Revelation is fulfilled or unfulfilled, if you consider the *man of sin* to be an individual, or if you believe prophetic days are years. About all these points you and I may be wrong, but still be saved. The one point I want you to nail down is this: Are you ready for the kingdom of Christ?

Do not tell me that by asking this I am setting too high a standard. It is pointless to tell me that a man may be a very good man but not yet be ready for the kingdom of Christ. I deny it altogether. I say that every justified and converted person is ready, and that if you are not ready, you are not a justified person. The standard I put before you is nothing more than the New Testament standard, and that the apostles would have doubted the truth of your religion if you were not looking and longing for the coming of the Lord. The grand end of the gospel is to prepare people to meet God. What has your Christianity done for you if it has not made you fit for the kingdom of Christ? Nothing! Nothing, nothing at all! Think about this and never rest until you are ready to meet Christ!

Now I offer an invitation to those who do not feel ready for Christ's return. It will be short and simple. I beg you to realize your danger and come to Christ without delay so you may be pardoned, justified, and made ready for the things to come. I plead with you to *flee from the wrath to come* (Matthew 3:7) and run to the hope set before you in the gospel. I ask you on Christ's behalf to lay down hostility and unbelief and be *reconciled to God* (2 Corinthians 5:20).

I tremble when I think of the privileges and opportunities that surround you in this country and of the danger you are in if you neglect them. I tremble when I think of the possibility of Christ coming again and of you being found unpardoned and unconverted in the day of His return. It will be a thousand times better to have been born a heathen and to have never heard the gospel than to have been a member of a church but not a living member of Christ. You have had enough time to delay taking care of the condition of your soul. Wake up! *Awake thou that sleepest, . . . and Christ shall give thee light* (Ephesians 5:14).

Lay aside everything that stands between you and Christ. Throw away everything that pulls you back and prevents you from feeling ready for the Lord's appearing. Find out the particular sin that weighs you down and tear it from your heart, however dear it may be. Cry fiercely to the Lord Jesus to reveal Himself to you. Do not rest until you have a real, firm, and reasonable hope, and know that your feet are on the Rock of Ages. Do not rest until you can say, "The Lord may come, the earth may be shaken, the foundations of the world may be turned upside down, but thank God I have treasure in heaven and an advocate with the Father, and I will not be afraid." Do this and you will have gotten something from this book.

Last, let me give an exhortation to all who truly know Christ and love His appearing. That exhortation is simply that you strive more and more to be a "doing" Christian (James 1:22). Work more and more to display the praises of Him who has called you out of darkness into marvelous light. Do everything you can to improve the gifts the Lord Jesus has given you to show His glory even better. Let your walk plainly declare that you *seek a country,* a homeland for eternity (Hebrews 11:14). Let your conformity to the mind of Christ be unquestionable and unmistakable. Let your holiness be so clear that even the worst enemies of the gospel cannot deny it.

> Let your holiness be so clear that even the worst enemies of the gospel cannot deny it.

Above all, if you are a student of prophecy, I ask you to never let your study prevent diligent, practical application. If you believe that the day is really approaching, then work to provoke others to love and good works. If you believe that the night is almost over, be doubly diligent to *cast off the works of darkness, and . . . put on the armour of light* (Romans 13:12). There is not a greater mistake than to imagine that the doctrine of the personal return of Christ is calculated to paralyze Christian diligence. Certainly there can be no greater spur to the servant's activity than the expectation of his master's speedy return.

This is the way to attain a healthy soul. There is nothing like practicing the fruit of the Spirit for promoting our spiritual strength. There are many of God's saints who complain that they lack spiritual comfort in their religion, but the fault is altogether in themselves. "Occupy, occupy," I would say to them. Zealously work for the glory of God and these uncomfortable feelings will soon vanish.

This is the way to do good to the children of the world. Nothing, except God, has such an effect on unconverted people as the sight of a real, thoroughly complete, live Christian. There are thousands who will not come to listen to the gospel and do not know the meaning of justification by faith, but who can understand an uncompromising, holy, consistent walk with God. "Occupy, occupy," I say, if you want to do good.

This is the way to promote fitness for the inheritance of the saints in light. There will be no idleness in the kingdom of Christ. The saints and angels there will wait on their Lord with unwearied activity and serve Him day and night. It is a fine saying of Bernard,[16] that Jacob in his vision saw some angels ascending and some descending, but none standing still. "Occupy, occupy," I say again, if you want to be thoroughly trained for your glorious home.

Oh fellow believers, it would be so good if we could see how much it is for our benefit and happiness to use every penny God gives us in living and striving to be near to God.

When we live like this, we will find great joy in our work, great comfort in our trials, great doors of usefulness in the world, great consolation in our sicknesses, great hope in our death, leave great evidence behind us when we are buried, have great confidence in the day of Christ's return, and receive a great crown in the day of reward.

---

16   Bernard of Clairvaux (1090–1153) was a medieval abbot and reformer.

Chapter 3

What Time Is It?

The night is far spent, the day is at hand: let us therefore cast off the works of darkness, and let us put on the armour of light. (Romans 13:12)

You probably know the story of Paul's shipwreck (Acts 27). You remember how the apostle and his companions were battered by a storm for thirteen days. Neither the sun nor the stars appeared for many days, and they gave up all hope that they would be saved. But do you remember that about midnight, on the fourteenth night, the shipmen sensed that they were approaching land? They measured and found the depth of the water to be twenty fathoms.[17] When they had gone a little farther, they measured again and found it to be fifteen fathoms. Then, afraid they might be dashed against the rocks near the shore, they dropped four anchors out of the stern and wished for day to come. Think what an anxious night that must have been! How often some of the 276 men on board the great Alexandrian ship must have said, "How much longer until morning? What time is it?"

You have probably heard of the Battle of Waterloo. You know that the Duke of Wellington fought that battle with the understanding that the Prussians would come up on the left of his army and help him against the French. But the way was long and the roads were bad. The

---

17   A fathom is equal to six feet and is used in reference to depth of water.

evening was coming before the Prussians could arrive at the field. In the meantime, the battle escalated. Hour after hour the British forces were thinned by the furious attacks of the enemy. One gallant man after another was killed or carried away wounded. Think what an anxious afternoon that must have been! How often the sun and the shadows must have been observed! How often the soldiers must have checked their watches and seen the general's eye turned to the left! How often the anxious question must have risen in men's minds, "What time is it?"

You have probably sat at the sickbed of some whom you dearly loved. You have seen them hovering between life and death and have passed weeks in painful suspense. You have sat by and watched the struggle between the body and its infirmities and felt the miserable helplessness of not being able to do anything but look on. And do you not know how slowly the hours roll around at a time like this? Have not the clocks and watches seemed to stand still, and the sun appeared to have forgotten to rise? Have you not often said, "When will the doctor come again? Will the morning never come? What time is it?"

> You and I are in a world that is rapidly rolling on towards the day of judgment.

You and I are in a world that is rapidly rolling on towards the day of judgment. There is an hour before us all when the earth and its works will be burned up and its inhabitants will all stand before the judgment seat of Christ. There is a day coming whose issues are of far more importance than those of shipwreck, battle, or disease. Surely it is appropriate for us to think of that day. Are we ready for it? Is it possible that we may live to see it? Is it near or is it far off? *What time is it?*

Come with me and consider the thoughts of an inspired apostle on this serious subject. He says, *The night is far spent, the day is at hand: let us therefore cast off the works of darkness, and let us put on the armour of light.* These words ought to awaken our consciences like the blast of a trumpet. They ought to rouse our sleeping minds to a sense of the eternal realities which are before us. They urge us to not delay or waste time or be careless about our Christianity. They summon us to a close walk with God.

Four questions are brought to mind by the words of this verse, and I will speak about each of these.

1. What is the present condition of the world?
2. What is the condition of the world that is coming?
3. What is the particular time in which we live?
4. What is the duty of all believers who know the time?

What is the present condition of the world?

The apostle Paul calls it *night*. *The night,* he says, *is far spent.* I do not doubt that word seems strange to some people. They think it wonderful that this year should be called *night*. They are living in days of learning, science, civilization, commerce, freedom, and knowledge. They see around them goods and experiences that their ancestors never dreamed of. I am aware of them all and am thankful for them. But I still say that in the things of God the world is in a state of night.

I believe that God looks down on this globe of ours as it rolls around the sun, and as He looks on it, He pronounces it "very dark."

I believe that the angels go back and forth reporting what they see on our earth and their constant report is, "Very dark."

And I am sure that believers in the Lord Jesus in every land are of one mind on this subject. They cry and sigh because of the abominations they see around them. To them the world appears very dark.

Is it not dark in heathen lands? Two-thirds of the whole world is in open rebellion against God and His Christ. Many of the world's inhabitants still have no Bible, no gospel, no knowledge, no faith, no hope. They are cruel, deceitful, immoral, unclean, earthly, sensual, devilish, idolatrous, and superstitious. Surely that is night.

Is it not dark in many countries that profess to be Christian? Many of the people on earth who call themselves Christians are unsound in their faith. Their religion is not solely scriptural. They have added to it many things that are not found in the Bible. They have left out of it many things that the Bible has plainly commanded. There are millions who give honor to the Virgin Mary and to dead saints instead of to Christ. There are millions of baptized people who know nothing of the Bible and have not the slightest idea of the salvation contained in the gospel. Certainly that is night.

Is it not dark in our own country in this present day? How much sin and how little of God! How much open infidelity, biblical ignorance, drunkenness, Sabbath-breaking, swearing, cheating, lying, and covetousness are weekly crying against us before the Lord of Hosts! Some go to church merely as a formality, and many go to no place of worship at all! How few are really earnest about the salvation of their souls! How few have any evidence to show of a saving faith in Christ and a real work of the Spirit in their hearts! Even among ourselves, it is night.

Go to what are considered to be the most godly cities and regions of the country and you will find that even there, very few people are truly converted Christians. If that is the case in the green and living parts, what must it be like in the dry and dead areas? Surely it is night.

It is useless to deny these things. Humbling as it may be to the pride of human nature, the word of the apostle is true – it is now night. The unconverted may not perceive it. Those without grace may not comprehend it. The blind eye sees no difference between noon and midnight. The deaf ear makes no distinction between discord and sweet music. The paralyzed limb has no feeling either of heat or cold. But I do believe that God's children can understand the expression. The people of the Lord Jesus Christ find by experience that it is night.

It is a cold time for believers. They meet with much to chill and dampen their zeal, but little to cheer and warm their hearts. They have to put up with many hardships and disappointments. They see sin abounding, and their own love is apt to become cold. Why? Because it is night.

It is a lonely time for believers. They find little company on the way that leads to heaven. Here and there they meet one who loves the Lord Jesus and lives by faith. A few of God's children may be found in one town and a few in another. But on the whole, the children of the world seem like the Syrian army which *filled the country* (1 Kings 20:27), and the children of God are like a few scattered sheep in a wilderness. And why? Because it is night.

It is a dangerous time for believers. They often stumble and can barely make out their path. They often stand in doubt and do not know which way to turn. They do not see their trail markers and lose sight of their landmarks. At best, they travel on in continual fear of enemies. Why? Because it is night.

I ask you to consider these things. If it is now night, you will not wonder why we warn Christians to watch and pray. You will not think it strange if we tell you to live like soldiers in an enemy's country and to be always on your guard.

Ask yourself if you find this world in which you live to be night or day. Is now a time of conflict or a time of ease? Do you feel that your best things are here in this life or that your best things are yet to come? I ask these questions so you can test your spiritual state. I set them before you as a gauge and measure of your soul's condition. If you have never found this world a wilderness and place of darkness, it is an evil sign of your state in the sight of God. True believers will find the words of their crucified Lord to be absolutely true: *In the world ye shall have tribulation* (John 16:33). True believers, like their Lord and Master, will be made *perfect through sufferings* (Hebrews 2:10). True believers will mourn over the world they live in as a world in rebellion against its rightful King. Sin will grieve them. Ungodliness will depress them. Like Lot in Sodom, their righteous souls will be frustrated daily with much that they see and hear. They will long for the time when the day will dawn and the shadows flee away. But for now, they will feel it is night. Is it your night or day?

What is the condition of the world that is coming?

The apostle Paul calls it *day. The day is at hand.* This day Paul speaks of is the time all Christians should look forward to – the time when the Lord Jesus Christ will come again.

The present state of things in the church of Christ will undergo a mighty change – a change so great that it will be like the turning of night into day. The world we live in will not always continue as it does now. The darkness of sin, ignorance, and superstition will not always cover the earth. The Sun of Righteousness will one day rise with healing in His wings. The Lord Jesus will come again with power and great glory. He will return as a morning without clouds, and then it will be day.

There is a time coming when the devil will be bound and will no longer rule this world (Revelation 20). Sin and all its consequences will be cast out. The groaning creation will at last be refreshed (Acts 3:19). The wicked will be imprisoned forever in their own place. The saints of the Most High will finally possess the kingdom. Righteousness will reside in a new heaven and a new earth. Certainly, that will be day.

There is a time coming when believers will have joy and gladness, and sorrow and sighing will flee far away. Every tear will be wiped away, every cross laid down, every anxiety removed, every adversity taken away. Persecution, temptation, sickness, mourning, parting, separation, and death will end. Surely that will be sunshine. It will be day.

There is a time coming when the whole family of Christ will be gathered together. They will rise from their narrow beds and each put on a glorious body. They will awake from their long sleep refreshed, strengthened, and far more beautiful than when they lay down. They will leave behind them in their graves every imperfection and will meet without spot or wrinkle (Ephesians 5:27) to part no more. That will be a joyful morning. It will be day.

There is a time coming when believers will no longer see through a glass darkly but face-to-face (1 Corinthians 13:12). They will see as they have been seen and know as they have been known. They will cease to argue and dispute about outward matters and will think of nothing but eternal realities. They will see their crucified Lord and Savior with literal sight and no longer follow Him by faith. They will see one another free from the stain of sin and will misunderstand one another's motives and conduct no more. Definitely, that will be day.

There is great comfort here for every believer in Christ. There is a day before you, a glorious day. You sometimes feel now as if you walk in darkness and have no light. You often have a hard battle to fight with the world, the flesh, and the devil. You sometimes believe you will never win your way home but will faint on the way. Your flesh and heart are ready to fail. You are painfully tempted to give up and to sit down in despair. But take comfort in the thought of things still to come. There is a good time in front of you. Your day has yet to dawn.

But for many of those who profess to be Christians, I also see here a great reason to be afraid. There are many, too many, I fear, for whom the time to come will be anything but day. There are many whose happiness is evidently all here below, whose treasure is all on earth, whose brightest time is now, and whose gloomiest prospects are in the hereafter. The further they look on, the darker everything appears. Old age looks dark, sickness looks darker still, death and judgment look darkest of all!

Oh friend, if this is how it is with you, I warn you that there must be a change. Your views, your tastes, your preferences, your attachments must be renewed and transformed. You must learn to view the present world and the world that is to come in a very different light. Go sit at the feet of Jesus and ask Him to teach you this lesson. Ask for the enlightening Spirit to anoint your eyes so that you can see. Ask for the veil to be taken away so that you may see everything in its true colors.

> I warn you that there must be a change.

Satan works hard to prevent people from thinking of a better world than that in which they now live. He strives to turn their eyes from the coming day. He gladly persuades them that it is impossible to live their lives in this world while setting their thoughts and affections on things above. He whispers to people that we ministers want them to become gloomy hermits or fanatical haters and cynics, and that if they listen to us they will become unfit for all of life's relationships. Be on guard against all of Satan's suggestions.

I am not asking you to neglect the duties of your occupation or the role God has called you to fill. I encourage no one to be rude and gloomy as if there were nothing to be thankful for in this world. I do not praise anyone who refuses to show love and affection to their family, friends, or other relationships. I only ask that believers in the New Testament live by a New Testament standard; they should look for the coming of the day of God, wait for the Son of God from heaven, and love the Lord's appearing.

I despise all fanatical absurdity on the subject of future things. I have no opinion of any religion which makes people neglect their business or cease to love their spouse, children, relatives, and friends. I only ask that we take scriptural views of the present things and things as they will one day be. I ask that we see our present evils and mourn over them and that we see and long for our future good things. Let us honestly acknowledge that sin is around us and let us long to be delivered from its presence. Let us honestly confess that holiness will one day spread over the earth and let us long for it to come. Never be ashamed to admit that it is night and that we want it to be day.

Can you really hate sin but not desire to see it swept away from the earth? Can you love holiness but not long for the time when all will know the Lord? Can you be truly united to Christ by faith but not wish to see Christ and be with Him? Can you be a saint and not thirst after the absolute fellowship of just people made perfect? Can you be sincere if you daily pray, *Thy kingdom come,* but are content if the world goes on as it is without any change? Oh no, no! These things are impossible. God's true children will want to be at home. They will wish for the day.

If you desire to be saved, you must learn to view the present time as night and the time to come as day. You must learn to regard the other side of Jordan as your true rest and home and this side as a desert land. Now is your wilderness, your battlefield, your place of trial. Your Canaan, your rest, your Father's house must be in the future, in the time to come – or else it will be better for you to have never been born.

What is the particular time in which we live?

The apostle Paul tells us when he says, *The night is far spent, the day is at hand.* I believe these words mean that the last order of things has arrived; the last stage in the history of the church has come. The law and the prophets have done their work. The Messiah promised at the fall has appeared and provided a complete salvation. The last revelation of God's will has been made. The way to life has been revealed clearly to all mankind. No further message from heaven to earth is to be expected before the end. No more books of Scripture are to be written. We have reached the last watch of the night. We have nothing to expect now but the sunrise and the morning.

These words, which were true thousands of years ago, are, if possible, more true at the present time. They are words which should hit home with increasing power to the church of Christ every year. *The night is far spent, the day is at hand.*

I am one of those who think the day may not be so far off as some suppose. Some say that the Lord's return in glory is an event that "of course" cannot be in our times, but I see tokens of the sun being near the horizon. In any event, I will keep first in my mind the words of James: *The coming of the Lord draweth nigh . . .the judge standeth before the door,* and the words of Peter: *The end of all things is at hand* (James 5:8-9; 1 Peter 4:7).

I am no prophet and may very well be mistaken. I may die, and you may die before Christ comes and the day dawns. But I ask every person to consider if there are signs of the times which deserve serious attention. I ask you to notice the things going on in the world and to give thought to what they are intended to teach.

What are these signs of the times? Consider the following points:

1. What do we say about the mission movements which have been initiated in these latter days? As late as the early 1800s, Protestant churches seemed thoroughly asleep on the subject of missions. Hardly a single missionary was sent from the whole of Great Britain; the idea of preaching the gospel to savages and idolaters was ridiculed. The first promoters of missions were treated coldly by many who ought to have known better, but now the feeling is completely changed. We employ hundreds of missionaries in every quarter of the globe. And the Scripture says, *This gospel of the kingdom shall be preached in all the world for a witness unto all nations; and then shall the end come* (Matthew 24:14).

2. What do we say to the surprising interest taken in the Jewish nation in these latter days? Just a while ago, to be a Jew was a taunt, a byword, a proverb. No one cared for the souls of the children of Abraham. They were a people despised and scorned and trampled underfoot. It could have truly been said, *This is Zion, whom no man seeketh after* (Jeremiah 30:17). But now the feeling is completely changed. The spiritual interests of Jews are a subject of deep concern to true Christians. The civil rights of Jews are cared for even to an extreme. The very city of Jerusalem has weight in the councils of kings. And the Scripture says, *Thou shalt arise, and have mercy upon Zion: for the time to*

favour her, yea, the set time, is come. For thy servants take pleasure in her stones, and favour the dust thereof. So the heathen shall fear the name of the LORD, *and all the kings of the earth thy glory. When the* LORD *shall build up Zion, he shall appear in his glory* (Psalm 102:13-16).

3. What will we say about the wonderful spread of knowledge and communication between nations in these days? Even in the early nineteenth century it was uncommon to find a poor man who could read, but now it seems to be a rare thing to find a man who cannot read. Then there were few that ever traveled outside their own country, but now everyone can move in every direction, and our population is like a disturbed swarm of bees. New modes of transportation have altered the character of society. Time and space are made nothing. Seas, mountains, and rivers are no longer obstacles. God separated the nations in the day of Babel; man is working hard to make them all one again. And what does the Scripture say? *Shut up the words, and seal the book, even to the time of the end: many shall run to and fro, and knowledge shall be increased* (Daniel 12:4).

4. What do we say about the wars and upheavals of nations which we have seen in these latter days? The mightiest empires on earth have been shaken to their very foundations. Kings, princes, and great men have been driven from their high positions and been made wanderers on the face of the earth. Human reasoning cannot explain it. These movements have taken place in the face of increased knowledge, civilization, and desire for peace. The shock came from beneath. The Scripture says, *Nation shall rise against nation, and kingdom against kingdom: and there shall be famines, and pestilences, and earthquakes, in divers places. All these are the beginning of sorrows* (Matthew 24:7-8).

5. What do we say about the drying up of Islamic power?[18]

---

18 In the seventeenth, eighteenth, and nineteenth centuries, the Muslim empires did experience a decline in power because of internal issues and the rise of power in Europe.

Several hundred years ago it was thought that the Turks were going to overrun all of Europe! No army seemed able to resist them. Province after province fell into their hands. When Martin Luther in his sermons wanted an illustration of boundless worldly power, he chose for his example "the Turkish empire"! But now all is changed. Without much outward violence Islamic strength has gradually dwindled away. There has been a collapse, a consumption, a worm at the heart of all their might. In spite of all the help from their allies, the Turkish empire is like a man sick of a distressing disease. He may rally for a time with the help of strong remedies and by the application of new elements and treatments into his body, but he will never again be an exclusive, persecuting, purely Muslim power. The days of pure, intolerant Islam seem past and gone forever. What does the Scripture say? I quote symbolic prophecy with reverence, and without hesitation I admit I may be wrong in its application. But the passage I refer to is very remarkable:

And the sixth angel poured out his vial upon the great river Euphrates; and the water thereof was dried up, that the way of the kings of the east might be prepared. And I saw three unclean spirits like frogs come out of the mouth of the dragon, and out of the mouth of the beast, and out of the mouth of the false prophet. For they are the spirits of devils, working miracles, which go forth unto the kings of the earth and of the whole world, to gather them to the battle of that great day of God Almighty. Behold, I come as a thief. Blessed is he that watcheth, and keepeth his garments, lest he walk naked, and they see his shame. (Revelation 16:12-15)

6. What do we say about the increased attention to unfulfilled prophecy that has emerged in these latter days? In the past there were few who paid any attention to the subject. The

passages in Scripture which speak of things to come were relatively neglected or perverted with unusual ingenuity from their simple meaning. Now, on the contrary, the current of public feeling runs strongly in favor of prophetic study. Books on the subject are eagerly bought up. Lectures on prophecy are listened to with increased attention. In spite of the divisions that some views have created, and in spite of the discredit that some groups have brought on the whole subject,[19] the study of unfulfilled prophecy still holds its ground. The Scripture says that *the words are closed up and sealed till the time of the end* (Daniel 12:9). The words seem to be unfolding and the seal seems to be breaking. Can the end be far off?

I place these points before you and ask you to give them your serious attention. I know we are all poor judges of our own times. We are apt to exaggerate the importance of events that take place in front of our own eyes. I dare say if we had lived in Cromwell's days or under the first French revolution, we would have thought the end of all things was close at hand. But even so, I think the points I have mentioned deserve sincere consideration. I see them as signs of our times.

There may still be sensational changes before the end comes. I think it is possible there may be yet a time of trouble and conflict *such as never was since there was a nation* (Daniel 12:1). I believe there may be tribulation for the people of God *such as was not since the beginning of the world* (Matthew 24:21). But whatever comes, I see deep meaning in the words, *The night is far spent, the day is at hand.*

In these words is the strongest motive for diligence in the work of doing good for people. More urgently spread the gospel over the world and work harder to sow the truth at home. Let us attempt to pluck more brands *out of the fire* (Zechariah 3:2). The time is short. The night is far spent. The day is at hand.

In these words is the strongest consolation for the believer in Christ Jesus. Oh, for the strength and desire to hold on to it tighter! In a little

---

19 Preterism, which sees the fulfillment of all prophecy in the past, and futurism, the view that places these events still in the future, were two prevailing views at the time this book was written. Some of the groups who damaged the study of prophecy were the Millerites in America and the Irvingites in England.

while believers will forever part with disease. The sick and weary ones who have mourned over their seeming uselessness to the church, the weak and infirm who have had the will to work but not the power, the feeble and bedridden who have waited long years in quiet bedrooms until their eyes know every crack and speck on their walls – all, all will be set free. They will each have a glorious body like their Lord's.

In a little while mourning believers will part forever with their tears. Every wound in their hearts will be completely healed. Every empty place and gap caused by death will be entirely filled up. They will find that those who have died in the Lord were not lost but gone ahead. They will see that infinite wisdom arranged every passing, by which one was taken and another left. They will magnify the Lord together with those who were once their companions in adversity, and acknowledge that He did all things well and led them in the right way.

> In a little while working believers will find that their labor was not in vain.

In a little while believers will no longer feel that they are alone. They will no longer be scattered over the earth, a few in one place and a few in another. They will no longer mourn that they see so few to speak to intimately, as a friend speaks with a friend, so few who are of one mind and travel with them in the one narrow way. They will be united with the general assembly and church of the firstborn. They will join the blessed presence of all the believers of every name, people, and tongue. Their eyes will at last truly see. They will see a multitude of saints, too many to count and not a wicked person among them.

In a little while working believers will find that their labor was not in vain. The ministers who preached and seemed to reap no fruit, the missionaries who testified of the gospel but none seemed to believe, the teachers who poured into children's minds but none seemed to pay attention – all, all will discover that they have not spent their strength in vain. They will find that the seed sown can spring up after many days, and that sooner or later in all labor there is profit.

Ah, but when will these things be? Truly we may say with Ezekiel, *O Lord God, thou knowest* (Ezekiel 37:3). A thousand years in His sight are as one day, and one day as a thousand years. But we do know that in just a little while He who is coming will come and will not delay. In a little while the last sermon will be preached, the last congregation will be dismissed. In a little while carelessness and infidelity will cease, perish, and pass away. The believers among us will be with Christ, and the unbelievers will be in hell. The night is far spent, and the day is at hand.

What is the duty of all believers who know the time?

That practical duty is stated in plain words: *Let us therefore cast off the works of darkness, and let us put on the armour of light.* The word *therefore* is often used by the apostle Paul in a very striking and forcible way. Look at a few examples and you will see what I mean.

When he finishes the doctrinal part of the epistle to the Romans and begins his practical teaching, what language does he use? *I beseech you **therefore**, brethren, by the mercies of God, that ye present your bodies a living sacrifice, holy, acceptable unto God* (Romans 12:1, emphasis added).

When he has preached the resurrection of the body to the Corinthians, how does he close his argument? ***Therefore,** my beloved brethren, be ye stedfast, unmoveable* (1 Corinthians 15:58, emphasis added).

When he has laid a powerful doctrinal foundation for the Ephesian church, how does he proceed to address them on practical duties? *I **therefore**, the prisoner of the Lord, beseech you that ye walk worthy of the vocation wherewith ye are called* (Ephesians 4:1, emphasis added).

And here, as in other places, the word *therefore* is used in a very searching and forcible way. *The night is far spent, the day is at hand: let us **therefore** cast off the works of darkness* (emphasis added).

I love to observe how closely the doctrine of Christ's second coming and kingdom is bound with personal holiness. I am astonished that any can regard the second advent and reign of the Lord Jesus as mere speculation or denounce them as unprofitable concerns. To me they seem extremely practical or else I have read my Bible without understanding and in vain.

The apostle Paul says to the Philippians, *Let your moderation be known unto all men. The Lord is at hand* (Philippians 4:5), and to the Colossians, *Set your affection on things above, not on things on the earth. For ye are dead, and your life is hid with Christ in God. When Christ, who is our life, shall appear, then shall ye also appear with him in glory. Mortify therefore your members which are upon the earth* (Colossians 3:2-5). He instructs the Hebrews to *exhort one another: and so much the more, as ye see the day approaching* (Hebrews 10:25). Peter tells his readers, *We, according to his promise, look for new heavens and a new earth, wherein dwelleth righteousness. Wherefore, beloved, seeing that ye look for such things, be diligent that ye may be found of him in peace, without spot, and blameless* (2 Peter 3:13-14). These texts appear to speak with a sure voice. I do not know how their force can be evaded. They make the coming of Christ and the day of glory an argument for increased holiness. And it is in the same way that Paul says, *Let us therefore cast off the works of darkness, and let us put on the armour of light.*

How are you to cast off the works of darkness? Listen to me and I will tell you. You need to lay aside everything in your life and habits which will not be able to stand the light of Christ's appearing. Make it a principle of conscience to do nothing you would not like to be found doing when Jesus comes again to gather His people together.

This is a probing and piercing test. The application of it must be left to every person's own heart. We must each judge for ourselves and prove our own works. You must set up court within yourself and honestly bring your ways to trial. Oh, for the will to deal fairly and justly with ourselves, and for a daily readiness to judge ourselves so that we will not be judged by the Lord, and to condemn ourselves so that we will not be condemned at the last day!

Shine the light of the day of Christ on your heart. Set your years, months, weeks, days, and hours in the full blaze of that day, and whatever you find that is related to darkness, pluck it out and throw it away. Keep no questionable habit. Do not compromise with doubtful practices. Break down every idol, great or small. Cut down every grove and clean the idols out of every room. Keep nothing that would cause you to blush with embarrassment under the eye of Christ. Do away with it at once, so that if He comes suddenly He will not put you to shame! May He never say of your heart in that day, "This heart claimed to be a temple of the Holy Spirit, but you have made it a den of thieves!"

Judge how you use your time by the test of Christ's second coming. Place in this balance your entertainment, your books, your companions, your conversation, your daily behavior in all areas of your life. Measure everything by this: *The night is far spent, the day is at hand,* and ask yourself, "Am I living as a child of the night or as one who looks for the day?" Do this and you will cast off the works of darkness.

But how are you to put on the armor of light? Listen to me once more, and I will tell you. You ought to aim for every grace and habit that suits a believer in Christ, a child of God, and a citizen of a heavenly kingdom. Do not leave notable holiness and spirituality to a few as if none but a few favored ones could be distinguished saints. You ought to strive to wear the armor of light, the belt of truth, the breastplate of righteousness, the helmet of salvation, and the sword of the Spirit yourself (Ephesians 6:14-17). Wherever you may live and whatever may be your trials – no matter how great your difficulties and small your help – nothing should prevent you from aiming at the highest standard and behaving like one who believes that Christ is coming again.

You should resolve, by God's help, to live so that the day of Christ will find you needing as little change as possible. You should seek to have tastes so heavenly, desires so spiritual, a will so subdued, and a mind so unworldly that when the Lord appears you will be thoroughly in tune for His kingdom. It was a fine saying of Dr. Preston on his deathbed: "I go to change my place, but not my company."[20]

I fear that some believers will be far less ready for the day of Christ than others who will have a far more abundant entrance into heaven. They will have more boldness and more confidence because they feel ready for the company of their Lord. I pray that everyone who reads this may walk with God in the same way, so that like Enoch, they are just transported from a lower level of communion to a higher one; they go from walking by faith to walking by sight. This would be putting on the armor of light.

Let there be light in your heart continually. Let Christ reside there by faith – felt, known, and experienced by your soul. Let there be light in your life continually. Let Christ be reflected there, followed, imitated, and copied. Seek to be a light in the world and nothing less, a bright and clear light that men can see from far away. Do this and you will put on the armor of light.

Live as if you think Christ might come at any time. Do everything

---

20   Dr. John Preston (1587–1628) was an Anglican pastor and an early Puritan.

as if it were for the last time. Say everything as if it were for the last time. Read every chapter in the Bible as if you do not know whether you will be allowed to read it again. Pray every prayer as if it might be your last opportunity. Listen to every sermon as if you are listening once and forever. This is the way to be found ready for Christ's second appearing. This is the way to put on the armor of light.

Perhaps you are an unconverted person who has given no thought or care to the Lord's coming. If so, then remember these words: *The night is far spent, the day is at hand.* What are you doing? You eat, you drink, you sleep, you dress, you work, you buy, you sell, you laugh, you read, but you do nothing for your soul. Hell is opening its mouth for you, and you do not care. Christ is coming to judge the world, and you are unprepared. Time hurries on, and you are not ready for eternity. Oh, awake to a sense of your danger and repent today! Awake and call upon your God before it is too late to pray. Awake and seek the Lord Jesus Christ before the door is shut and the day of wrath begins. You may be considered wise and clever in this world, but you are living as a lunatic.

> Awake and seek the Lord Jesus Christ before the door is shut and the day of wrath begins.

But perhaps you are undecided and wavering between belief and unbelief. If this is you, then remember these words: *The night is far spent, the day is at hand.*

What are you doing? You hear, you listen, you wish, you desire, you mean, you intend, you hope, you resolve, but you go no further. You see the ark, but you will not go in. You see the Bread of Life, but you do not eat it. You wait. And time goes on. The devil is saying over you, "I will have this soul before long." Oh, come out from the world and procrastinate no more! Take up the cross. Cast away vain excuses. Confess Christ before men. Be careful that you do not make up your mind too late.

Perhaps you are a true believer. Then remember these words: *The night is far spent, the day is at hand.* I ask you to live as if you believed the words we have been considering and to show the world you think they are true. The closer you get to home, the more awake you ought to be. The more you understand the second personal coming of the Lord Jesus, the more lively your Christianity should be.

It is too true. As Legh Richmond said on his deathbed, "We are but half awake! We are but half awake!" Even the best of us need reminders. Let us rub the sleepy eyes of our mind and look the speedy coming of our Master full in the face. We have spent enough time being drowsy and lazy servants. Now let us work like those who believe that the Master will soon be here.

When I was a schoolboy, I remember that I could wake up, no matter how tired from a long journey, when I began to get close to home. As soon as I saw the old hills and trees and chimneys, the sense of weariness was gone, and I was all alive. The prospect of soon seeing much-loved faces, the joy of thinking of a family gathering – these were able to drive sleep away. Surely it ought to be the same with us in the matter of our souls. The night is far spent, and the day is at hand. In a little while, He who is coming will come and will not tarry. So let us cast off every work of darkness. Let us put on the whole armor of light. Let us be ashamed of our past drowsiness. Let us awake and sleep no more.

"Soon and Forever"

Soon and forever, the breaking of day
    Shall chase all the night-clouds of sorrow away
Soon and forever, we'll see as we're seen,
    And know the deep meaning of things that have been.
Where fightings without and conflicts within
    Shall weary no more in the warfare with sin,
Where tears and where fears and where death shall be never,
    Christians with Christ shall be soon and forever!

Soon and forever, such promise our trust,
    Though ashes to ashes, and dust be to dust,
Soon and forever, our union shall be
    Made perfect, our glorious Redeemer, in Thee;
When the cares and the sorrows of time shall be o'er,
    Its pangs and its partings remembered no more,

Where life cannot fail and where death cannot sever,
    Christians with Christ shall be soon and forever!

Soon and forever, the work shall be done,
    The warfare accomplished, the victory won;
Soon and forever, the soldier lay down
    The sword for a harp, the cross for a crown;
Then droop not in sorrow, despond not in fear,
    A glorious tomorrow is brightening and near,
When, blessed reward for each faithful endeavor,
    Christians with Christ shall be soon and forever!
        — John S. B. Monsell

"Come, Lord, and Tarry Not"

Come Lord, and tarry not;
    Bring the long looked-for day;
Oh, why these years of waiting here,
    These ages of delay?

Come, for Thy saints still wait;
    Daily ascends their sigh;
The Spirit and the Bride say, Come,
    Dost Thou not hear the cry?

Come, for Thy Israel pines,
    An exile from Thy fold;
Oh, call to mind Thy faithful word,
    And bless them as of old!

Come, for the good are few;
    They lift their voice in vain;
Faith waxes fainter on the earth,
    And love is on the wane.

Come, for the corn is ripe;
    Put in Thy sickle now,
Reap the great harvest of the earth,
    Sower and Reaper Thou!

Come in Thy glorious might,
    Come with the iron rod,
Scattering Thy foes before Thy face,
    Most Mighty Son of God.

Come, and make all things new,
    Build up this ruined earth,
Restore our faded Paradise,
    Creation's second birth.

Come, and begin Thy reign
    Of everlasting peace;
Come, take the kingdom to Thyself,
    Great King of righteousness.
              — Horatius Bonar

Chapter 4

Idolatry to Be Destroyed at Christ's Coming

The idols he shall utterly abolish. (Isaiah 2:18)

To all who interpret the prophecy of Isaiah literally, the time spoken of here in Isaiah will be plain. It is the second coming of our Lord Jesus Christ, the day *when he ariseth to shake terribly the earth* (Isaiah 2:21). The event is part of the powerful purification which will then take place in His professing church – the abolishing of all idols. From this text, we will consider the subject of idolatry.

Let us look at four questions relating to idolatry.

1. What is it? What is the definition of idolatry?

2. Where does it come from? What is the cause of idolatry?

3. Where is it? What form does it take in the visible church of Christ?

4. What will end it? What will be the ultimate abolition of idolatry?

This subject of idolatry is a complicated one. We live in an age when truth is constantly in danger of being sacrificed to toleration, charity, and so-called peace. Nevertheless, I cannot forget that I am a minister of a church that has spoken plainly on the subject of idolatry, and unless

I am greatly mistaken, truth about idolatry is in the highest sense truth for the times.

What is it?

Let me first give you the definition of idolatry. It is of the utmost importance that you know what it is. Unless I make this clear, I can do nothing with the text. Vagueness and ambiguity prevail on this point as on almost every other topic in religion. To keep from running aground on their spiritual voyage, Christians must have their pathways well marked, and their minds filled with clear definitions.

My definition of idolatry is a worship in which the honor due to the Lord, and to Him only, is given to some of His creatures or some invention of His creatures. It may vary to a great extent. It may assume exceedingly different forms, according to the ignorance or the knowledge or the civilization of those who offer it. It may be grossly absurd and ludicrous or it may border closely on truth and be erroneously defended. But whether in the adoration of the idol of Juggernaut[21] or in the adoration of the host in St. Peter's at Rome, the idolatrous principle is the same. In either case the honor due to God is turned from Him and given to that which is not God. And whenever this is done, whether in heathen temples or in professedly Christian churches, this is idolatry.

You must bear in mind that it is not necessary for a man to formally deny God and Christ in order to be an idolater. Far from it. Professed reverence for the God of the Bible and actual idolatry are perfectly compatible. They have often gone side by side, and they still do so. The children of Israel never thought of renouncing God when they persuaded Aaron to make the golden calf. *These be thy gods* [thy Elohim], they said, *which brought thee up out of the land of Egypt.* And the feast in honor of the calf was kept as *a feast to the* LORD [Jehovah] (Exodus 32:4-5). Jeroboam never pretended to ask the ten tribes to

---

21   Juggernaut was a Hindu deity that became, in the West, the representation of all Indian gods.

cast off their allegiance to the God of David and Solomon. When he set up the calves of gold in Dan and Bethel he only said, *It is too much for you to go up to Jerusalem: behold thy gods* [thy Elohim], *O Israel, which brought thee up out of the land of Egypt* (1 Kings 12:28). In both instances you will observe that the idol was not set up as a rival to God, but under the pretense of being a help – a stepping-stone to His service. But in both instances a great sin was committed. The honor due to God was given to a visible representation of Him. The majesty of Jehovah was offended. The second commandment was broken. There was, in the eyes of God, a flagrant act of idolatry.

Recognize this and dismiss from your minds those loose and careless ideas about idolatry which are common today. Do not think that there are only two sorts of idolatry – the spiritual idolatry of people who love their spouse or child or money more than God, and the open, shameless idolatry of those who bow down to an image of wood, metal, or stone because they know no better. You can be sure that idolatry is a sin that occupies a far, far wider field than this. It is not merely a thing in India that you hear of and pity at missionary meetings, nor is it just a thing confined to your own heart that you can confess on your knees before the mercy seat. It is a pestilence that walks in the church of Christ to a much greater extent than many of you suppose. It is an evil that, like the man of sin, *sitteth in the temple of God* (2 Thessalonians 2:4). It is a sin that we all need to watch and pray against continually. It creeps stealthily into our religious worship and is upon us before we are even aware. Isaiah spoke these words not to the worshipper of Baal, but to the formal Jew who actually came to the temple: *He that killeth an ox is as if he slew a man; he that sacrificeth a lamb, as if he cut off a dog's neck; he that offereth an oblation, as if he offered swine's blood; he that burneth incense, as if he blessed an idol* (Isaiah 66:3).

Remember, God has specially denounced this sin of idolatry in His Word. One commandment out of ten is devoted to the prohibition of it. None of all the ten contain such a solemn declaration of His character and of His judgments against the disobedient: *I the* Lord *thy God am a jealous God, visiting the iniquity of the fathers upon the children unto the third and fourth generation of them that hate me* (Exodus 20:5). This commandment is emphatically repeated and amplified, especially in the fourth chapter of the book of Deuteronomy.

This is the sin that has brought down the heaviest judgments on the visible church. It brought on Israel the armies of Egypt, Assyria, and Babylon. It scattered the ten tribes, burned up Jerusalem, and carried Judah and Benjamin into captivity. Later, it brought on the Eastern churches the overwhelming flood of the Saracenic[22] invasion and turned many a spiritual garden into a wilderness. The desolation which reigns where Cyprian and Augustine[23] once preached, and the living death in which the churches of Asia Minor and Syria are buried are all attributable to this sin. All testify to the same great truth that the Lord proclaims in Isaiah: *My glory will I not give to another* (Isaiah 42:8).

Gather these things in your mind. Be very sure that every church of Christ that desires to stay pure needs to thoroughly examine, know, and understand the subject of idolatry.

Where does it come from?

Now let us discuss the cause of idolatry. Where does it come from? To the person who takes an exalted view of human intellect and reason, idolatry may seem absurd. He imagines it to be too irrational to be a danger to any but those with slow and weak minds. To someone who thinks only superficially about Christianity, the peril of idolatry may seem very small. This person will tell you that while professing Christians may break some of the commandments, the second commandment is not very likely to be one of them.

Now these people show a woeful ignorance of human nature. They do not see that there are secret roots of idolatry in all of us. The prevalence of idolatry in all ages among the heathen inevitably puzzles the one, and the warnings of Protestant ministers against idolatry in the church appear uncalled for to the other, since both are blind to its cause.

The cause of all idolatry is the natural corruption of man's heart. That great family disease, with which all the children of Adam are

---

22 Saracens was a term used to refer to people, primarily Muslim, from the tribes of Arabia.
23 Cyprian and Augustine were early church theologians and writers. They both lived in the area of North Africa.

born, shows itself in this, as it does in a thousand other ways. Out of the same fountain from which *proceed evil thoughts, adulteries, fornications, murders, thefts, covetousness, wickedness, deceit,* and the like (Mark 7:21-22) – out of that same fountain flow false views of God and false views of the worship due Him. Therefore, when the apostle Paul lists for the Galatians *the works of the flesh,* he places idolatry prominently among them (Galatians 5:20).

All people will have a religion of some kind. God has not left Himself without a witness in us all, fallen as we are. Like old inscriptions hidden under mounds of rubbish, like the almost-obliterated underwriting of palimpsest[24] manuscripts, there is a dim something engraved at the bottom of our hearts, however faint and half-erased – a something which makes us feel we must have a religion and a worship of some kind. The proof of this is to be found in the history of voyages and travels in every part of the globe. The exceptions to the rule are so few, if indeed there are any, that they only confirm its truth. It may be in some dark corners of the earth that the worship rises no higher than a vague fear of an evil spirit and a desire to win his favor, but a worship of some kind we will have.

But then the effects of the fall come into play. Ignorance of God, carnal and low regard of His nature and attributes, earthly and physical notions of the service which is acceptable to Him – all characterize the religion of natural man. There is a craving in our minds for something we can see and feel and touch in his divinity. We would gladly bring our God down to our own crawling levels. We would make our religion a thing of sense and sight. In our natural state, we have no idea of faith and spirit. Just as we, until renewed by grace, are willing to live a fallen and degraded life on God's earth, so until we are renewed by the Holy Spirit, we have no objection to worship in the same fallen way. Idolatry is a natural product of man's heart. It is a weed, which, like the earth uncultivated, the heart is always ready to bring out.

Does it surprise you when you read of the constantly recurring idolatries of the Old Testament church – of Peor and Baal and Moloch and Chemosh and Ashtoreth and of high places and hill altars and groves

---

24 A palimpsest is a page from a scroll or book that has been reused after the original text was washed off or erased.

and images – and this in the full light of the Mosaic law? Do not be surprised. It can be accounted for. There is a cause.

Does it surprise you when you read in history of idolatry creeping by degrees into the church of Christ – how little by little it thrust out gospel truth, until in Canterbury, men offered more at the shrine of Thomas Becket[25] than they did at that of the Virgin Mary, and more at that of the Virgin Mary than at that of Christ? Do not be surprised. It is all intelligible. There is a cause.

Does it surprise you when you hear of people today going over from Protestant churches to the Church of Rome? Do you find it inexplicable and feel that you could never trade a pure form of worship for one like that of the pope's? Do not be surprised. There is a solution. There is a cause.

And that cause is the deep corruption of man's heart. There is a natural inclination and tendency in us all to give God a physical, carnal worship, and not that which is commanded in His Word. We are ever ready to create for our sloth and unbelief visible helps and stepping-stones in our approach to Him, and ultimately to give these inventions of our own the honor due Him. In fact, idolatry is all natural, downhill, and easy like the broad way. Spiritual worship is all of grace, all uphill, and all against the grain. Any other kind of worship is more pleasing to the natural heart than worshipping God in the way our Lord Christ describes, *in spirit and in truth* (John 4:23).

I am not surprised at the quantity of idolatry existing both in the world and in the visible church. I believe it is perfectly possible that we may live to see even more of it than some have ever dreamed of. It would not surprise me if some powerful, personal antichrist were to arise before the end – mighty in intellect, mighty in talents for government, and perhaps mighty in miraculous gifts too. It would not surprise me to see such a person setting himself up in opposition to Christ and making an infidel combination against the gospel. I believe that many who now glory in saying, "We will not have this Christ to reign over us" would rejoice to give him honor. I believe that many would make a god of him and revere him as an incarnation of truth and concentrate their idea of hero worship on him. I suggest it as a possibility and no

---

25 Thomas Becket (c. 1119–1170), archbishop of Canterbury, was murdered by knights loyal to King Henry II.

more. But I am certain of this: no man is in more danger of idolatry than the man who now sneers at every form of religion; and that from unbelief to belief, and from atheism to the most blatant idolatry there is but a single step. Do not think that idolatry is an old-fashioned sin into which you are never likely to fall. *Wherefore let him that thinketh he standeth take heed lest he fall* (1 Corinthians 10:12). Look into your own hearts. The seeds of idolatry are all there.

Where is it?

What forms has idolatry assumed in the visible church? Where is it? Many believe that the promises of perpetuity, lasting forever, and the preservation from apostasy belong to the visible church of Christ. I believe there never was a more baseless idea than this theory. It is supported neither by Scripture nor by facts. The church against which the gates of hell will never prevail is not the visible church but the whole body of the elect, the company of true believers out of every nation and people. The greater part of the visible church has frequently maintained glaring heresies. The particular branches of it are never secure against deadly error, both of faith and practice. A departure from the faith, a falling away, a leaving of the first love in any branch of the visible church should never surprise a careful reader of the New Testament.

That idolatry would arise seems to have been the expectation of the apostles even before the canon of the New Testament was closed. It is remarkable to observe how Paul dwells on this subject in his epistle to the Corinthians. The members of the church in Corinth were not even to eat with one who claimed to be a brother but was an idolater (1 Corinthians 5:11). *Neither be ye idolaters, as were some of them* (1 Corinthians 10:7). He says again, *My dearly beloved, flee from idolatry* (1 Corinthians 10:14). When he writes to the Colossians, he warns them against the *worshipping of angels* (Colossians 2:18). And John closes his first epistle with the solemn warning: *Little children, keep yourselves from idols* (1 John 5:21). It is impossible not to feel that all these passages imply an expectation that idolatry would emerge among professing Christians and that it would happen soon.

The famous prophecy in the fourth chapter of the first epistle to Timothy contains a passage which is even more directly to the point: *Now the Spirit speaketh expressly, that in the latter times some shall depart from the faith, giving heed to seducing spirits, and doctrines of devils* (1 Timothy 4:1). I will not make a lengthy discussion of that remarkable expression, *doctrines of devils*. It will be sufficient to say that our excellent translators for once missed the full meaning of the apostle in their translation of the word stated in our version as *devils*. The true meaning of the expression is "doctrines about departed spirits." In this view, which is maintained by those most qualified to speak on this subject, the passage becomes a direct prediction of the rise of that most deceptive form of idolatry, the worship of dead saints.

The last passage I will call your attention to is the conclusion of the ninth chapter of Revelation, verse 20: *The rest of the men which were not killed by these plagues yet repented not of the works of their hands, that they should not worship devils* [this is the same word as that just quoted in the epistle to Timothy], *and idols of gold, and silver, and brass, and stone, and of wood: which neither can see, nor hear, nor walk*. I am not going to offer any comment on the chapter in which this verse occurs. I know very well there is a difference of opinion as to the true interpretation of the plagues predicted in it. One thing I dare to argue is that there is the highest probability these plagues are to fall on the visible church of Christ and the highest improbability that John was prophesying about the heathen who never heard the gospel. If you concede this, the fact that idolatry is a predicted sin of the visible church does seem most conclusively and continually established.

And now if we turn from the Bible to things that are known, what do we see? Unhesitatingly I reply that there is unmistakable proof that Scripture warnings and predictions were not spoken without cause, and that idolatry has emerged in the visible church of Christ and still exists.

You will find a good summary of the rise and progress of evil in former days in the admirable homily of our own church, "Against Peril of Idolatry."[26] I refer you to that homily and remind you once for all

---

26 The *Book of Homilies* are two books of the authorized sermons of the Church of England.

that in the judgment of your own Thirty-Nine Articles,[27] the *Book of Homilies* "contains a godly and wholesome doctrine, and necessary for these times." There you will read how, even in the fourth century, Jerome complains "that the errors of images have come in, and passed to the Christians from the gentiles"; and Eusebius says, "We do see now that images of Peter and Paul, and of our Savior Himself be made, and tables be painted, which I think to have been derived and kept indifferently by an heathenish custom." There you will also read that in the fifth century, "Pontius Paulinus, Bishop of Nola, caused the walls of the temples to be painted with stories taken out of the Old Testament; that the people beholding and considering these pictures, might the better abstain from too much surfeiting and riot. But from learning by painted stories, it came by little and little to idolatry." There you will read that in the beginning of the seventh century, Pope Gregory I, bishop of Rome, did allow images in churches, and that in the eighth century, Irene, mother of Constantine VI, assembled a council at Nicaea and was able to obtain a decree that images should be put up in all the churches of Greece, and that honor and worship should be given to the said images. And there you will read how the homily concludes its historical summary: "that laity and clergy, learned and unlearned, all ages, sorts, and degrees of men, women, and children of whole Christendom, have been at once drowned in abominable idolatry, of all other vices most detested of God, and most damnable to man, and that by the space of eight hundred years and more."

This is a sorrowful account, but it is only too true. There can be little doubt that the evil began even before the time mentioned by the homily writers. No one who calmly considers the excessive reverence which the early church paid from the very first to the visible parts of religion should be surprised by the vice of idolatry in the primitive church. I believe that no one can impartially read the language used by nearly all the church fathers about the church, the bishops, the ministry, baptism, the Lord's Supper, the martyrs, the dead saints generally – without being struck with the wide difference between their language and the language of Scripture on these subjects. You seem at once to be in a new

---

27 The Thirty-Nine Articles are part of the *Book of Common Prayer* and are the essential beliefs, the doctrinal statement, of the Anglican Church.

atmosphere. You feel that you are no longer treading on holy ground. You find things which in the Bible are evidently of second-rate importance, but are here made to be of first-rate importance. You find the things of sense and sight exalted to a position in which Paul and Peter and James and John, speaking by the Holy Spirit, never for a moment placed them. It is not merely the weakness of uninspired writings, it is also something worse. It is a new system. And what is the explanation of all this? It is that you are in a region where the malaria of idolatry began to arise. You perceive the first workings of the mystery of iniquity. You detect the buds of that huge system of idolatry which, as the homily describes, was afterwards formally acknowledged and ultimately blossomed so profusely in every part of Christendom.

But let us now turn from the past to the present. Let us examine the question that most concerns us: In what form does idolatry present itself to us as a sin of the visible church of Christ in our own time?

I can easily answer this question. I feel no hesitation in affirming that idolatry assumes its most glaring form in the Church of Rome at this very day.

This is a subject on which it is hard to speak because of the times we live in. But the whole truth ought to be spoken by ministers of Christ without respect to times or prejudices. After preaching on idolatry, I could not lie down in peace if I did not declare my conviction that idolatry is one of the crying sins of the Church of Rome. I say this in all sadness. I say it, acknowledging fully that we have our faults in our own church and practically, in some quarters, our own idolatry. But I believe we are free from formal, recognized, and systematic idolatry, while, as for the Church of Rome, if there is not an enormous quantity of systematic, organized idolatry in her worship, I frankly confess I do not know what idolatry is.

To my mind, it is idolatry to have images and pictures of saints in churches and to give them a reverence for which there is no warrant or precedent in Scripture. If this be so, I say there is idolatry in the Church of Rome.

To my mind, it is idolatry to invoke the Virgin Mary and the saints in glory and to address them in language never used in Scripture except to the Lord. And if this be so, I say there is idolatry in the Church of Rome.

To my mind, it is idolatry to bow down to mere material things and attribute to them a power and sanctity far exceeding that attached to the ark or altar of the Old Testament, and a power and sanctity, too, for which there is not a hint of foundation in the Word of God. And if this be so – with the holy coat of Treves,[28] and the amazingly multiplied wood of the true cross, and a thousand other so-called relics, I say there is idolatry in the Church of Rome.

> It is idolatry to invoke the Virgin Mary and the saints in glory and to address them in language never used in Scripture except to the Lord.

To my mind, it is idolatry to worship that which man's hands have made – to call it God and adore it when lifted up before our eyes. And if this be so, with the doctrine of transubstantiation[29] and the elevation of the host in my mind, I say there is idolatry in the Church of Rome.

To my mind, it is idolatry to make ordained men mediators between ourselves and God, robbing, as it were, our Lord Christ of His office, and giving them an honor which even apostles and angels in Scripture flatly refused. And if this be so, with the honor paid to popes and priests before my eyes, I say there is idolatry in the Church of Rome.

I know that language like this jolts the minds of many. Some love to shut their eyes against evil which is unpleasant to acknowledge. They will not see things which involve unpleasant consequences. That the Church of Rome is an erring church, they will acknowledge. That she is idolatrous, they will deny.

They tell us that the reverence that the Catholic Church gives to saints and images does not amount to idolatry. They inform us that there are distinctions between "latria" and "dulia,"[30] between a mediation of redemption and a mediation of intercession, which clear her of the charge. My reply is that the Bible knows nothing of such distinctions and that in the actual practice of the majority of Roman Catholics, they have no existence at all.

They tell us that it is a mistake to say that Roman Catholics really worship the images and pictures before which they perform acts of

---

28   The coat of Treves was believed to be the robe Jesus wore at the crucifixion.
29   Transubstantiation is the belief of the conversion of the elements of communion into the blood and body of Christ.
30   Latria is worship given to God alone and dulia is the respect given to angels and saints.

adoration. They say that they only use them as helps to devotion, and in reality, look far beyond them. My answer is that many heathens could say just as much for their idolatry; it is well known that in former days they did say so, and that in India many idol worshippers do say so in the present day. But the apology does not help. The terms of the second commandment are too stringent. It prohibits bowing down as well as worshipping. And the very anxiety which the Church of Rome has often displayed to exclude that second commandment from her catechisms is of itself a great fact which speaks volumes to a candid observer.

They tell us that we have no evidence for our assertions, that we base our charges on the abuses which prevail among the ignorant members of the church community, and that it is absurd to say that a church containing so many wise and learned men is guilty of idolatry. My answer is that the devotional books in common use among Roman Catholics supply us with unmistakable evidence. If you doubt my assertion, examine that notorious book, *The Garden of the Soul*,[31] and read the language there addressed to the Virgin Mary. Remember that this language is addressed to a woman who, though highly favored and the mother of our Lord, was yet a fellow sinner and actually confesses her need of a Savior for herself. She says, *My spirit hath rejoiced in God my Saviour* (Luke 1:47). Examine this language in the light of the New Testament and then tell us fairly if the charge of idolatry is not fully made. But in addition, what is done in the city of Rome itself supplies the best evidence. What do men and women do under the light of the pope's own presence? What is the religion that prevails around St. Peter's and within the walls of the Vatican? What is Roman Catholicism in Rome – unfettered, unshackled, and free to develop itself in full perfection? Honestly answer these questions, and I will not ask any more. Read a book such as Seymour's *A Pilgrimage to Rome* or Alford's *Letters from Abroad*,[32] and ask any visitor to Rome if the picture is too highly colored. Do this, I say, and I believe you cannot avoid the conclusion that Roman Catholicism in perfection is a gigantic system of Mary worship,

---

31 *The Garden of the Soul, or a Manual of Spiritual Exercises and Instructions for Christians Who Aspire to Devotion*, by Richard Challoner, 1775.
32 *Letters from Abroad* by Henry Alford, and *A Pilgrimage to Rome* by Michael Hobart Seymour.

saint worship, image worship, relic worship, and priest worship; that briefly, it is a huge organized idolatry.

I do not know how these things sound to your ears. I gain no pleasure thinking about the shortcomings of any who profess to be and call themselves Christians. I can truly say that I have said what I have said with pain and sorrow.

I draw a wide distinction between the Church of Rome and the private opinions of many of her members. I believe and hope that many Roman Catholics are in their heart inconsistent with what they profess and are better than the church to which they belong. I cannot forget the Jansenists and Pasquier Quesnel and Martin Boos.[33] I believe that many a poor Italian today is worshipping with an idolatrous worship simply because he does not know any better. He has no Bible to instruct him. He has no faithful minister to teach him. He has the fear of the priest before his eyes if he dares to think for himself. He has no money to enable him to get away from the bondage he lives under, even if he feels a desire to do so. I remember all this and say that the Italians very much deserve our sympathy and compassion, but all this must not prevent my saying that the Church of Rome is an idolatrous church.

If I said less, I would not be faithful. The church of which I am a minister has spoken out most strongly on the subject. The "Homily on Peril of Idolatry" and the words we declare following the rubrics[34] at the end of our communion service denouncing the adoration of the sacramental bread and wine as "idolatry to be abhorred of all faithful Christians" are plain evidence that I have told you just what my own church teaches. Today when some are disposed to break away and join the Church of Rome, and many are shutting their eyes to her real character and wanting us to be reunited to her – in a day like this, my own conscience would rebuke me if I did not warn men plainly that the Church of Rome is an idolatrous church and that if they will join her, they are "joining themselves to idols."

I will not spend any more time on this subject. The main point I want you to see is that idolatry has decidedly demonstrated itself in the visible church of Christ and nowhere so decidedly as in the Church of Rome.

33　These were Roman Catholics who emphasized justification by faith.
34　The rubrics are directions for what to do during worship and in other parts of the service.

What will end it?

The last thing I will address is the ultimate abolition of all idolatry. What will end it?

It is an unhealthy soul that does not long for a time when idolatry will be no more. That heart cannot be right with God that can think of the millions who are sunk in heathenism or honor the false prophet Muhammad or daily invoke the Virgin Mary and not cry, "O my God, what will be the end of these things? How long, O Lord? How long?" Here, as in other subjects, the sure word of prophecy comes to our aid. The end of all idolatry will one day come. Its doom is fixed. Its overthrow is certain. Whether in heathen temples or in so-called Christian churches, idolatry will be destroyed at the second coming of our Lord Christ.

Then the prophecy of our text will be fulfilled: *The idols he shall utterly abolish.* The prophecies of Micah, Zephaniah, and Zechariah will be realized: *Thy graven images also will I cut off, and thy standing images out of the midst of thee, and thou shalt no more worship the work of thine hands* (Micah 5:13); *The LORD will be terrible unto them: for he will famish all the gods of the earth; and men shall worship him, every one from his place, even all the isles of the heathen* (Zephaniah 2:11); *It shall come to pass in that day, saith the LORD of hosts, that I will cut off the names of the idols out of the land, and they shall no more be remembered* (Zechariah 13:2). Psalm 97 will at that time be fully and completely accomplished:

> *The LORD reigneth; let the earth rejoice; let the multitude of isles be glad thereof. Clouds and darkness are round about him: righteousness and judgment are the habitation of his throne. A fire goeth before him, and burneth up his enemies round about. His lightnings enlightened the world: the earth saw, and trembled. The hills melted like wax at the presence of the LORD, at the presence of the Lord of the whole earth. The heavens declare his righteousness, and all the people see*

his glory. Confounded be all they that serve graven images, that boast themselves of idols: worship him, all ye gods.

The coming and kingdom of our Lord Jesus Christ is the blessed hope which should always comfort the children of God until He does return. It is the guiding light by which we must journey. It is the one point on which all our expectations should be concentrated. *Yet a little while, and he that shall come will come, and will not tarry* (Hebrews 10:37). Our David will no longer dwell in Adullam, followed by a despised few and rejected by the many. He will take to Himself His great power and reign and cause every knee to bow before Him.

Until then our redemption is not perfectly enjoyed; as Paul tells the Ephesians, *[We] are sealed unto the day of redemption* (Ephesians 4:30). Our salvation is not completed. Peter says, *[We] are kept by the power of God through faith unto salvation ready to be revealed in the last time* (1 Peter 1:5). Our knowledge is still defective. Paul tells the Corinthians, *Now we see through a glass, darkly; but then face to face: now I know in part; but then shall I know even as also I am known* (1 Corinthians 13:12). In short, our best things are yet to come.

But in the day of our Lord's return every desire will be satisfied. We will no more be pressed down and worn out with the sense of constant failure, feebleness, and disappointment. In His presence we will find a fullness of joy that we have never had anywhere else, and when we wake up in His likeness we will be satisfied as we have never been before.

There are many abominations within the visible church over which we can only sigh and cry, like the faithful in Ezekiel's day (Ezekiel 9:4). We cannot remove them. But a day is coming when Jesus will once more purify His temple and cast forth everything that defiles it. He will do the work of which the actions of Hezekiah and Josiah were a faint type long ago. He will cast down the image and purge out idolatry in every shape.

Do you long for the conversion of the heathen world? You will not see it in its fullness until the Lord's appearing. Then, and not until then, will that often misapplied text be fulfilled: *A man shall cast his idols of silver, and his idols of gold, which they made each one for himself to worship, to the moles and to the bats* (Isaiah 2:20).

Do you long for the redemption of Israel? You will never see it in its perfection until the Redeemer comes to Zion. Idolatry in the professing church of Christ has been one of the mightiest stumbling blocks in the way of Jewish conversion. When it begins to fall, the veil over the heart of Israel will begin to be taken away (Psalm 102:16).

Do you long for the fall of antichrist and the purification of the Church of Rome? I believe that will never be until this dispensation comes to an end. That vast system of idolatry may be depleted and weakened by the spirit of the Lord's mouth, but it will never be destroyed except by the brightness of His coming (2 Thessalonians 2:8).

Do you long for a perfect church – a church in which there will not be the slightest taint of idolatry? You must wait for the Lord's return. Then, and not until then, will we see a perfect church – a church having neither spot nor wrinkle, nor any such thing (Ephesians 5:27) – a church of which all the members will be regenerate and every one a child of God.

If these things are true, you will not wonder why we urge you to study prophecy and that we charge you above all else to hold firmly to the glorious doctrine of Christ's second appearing and kingdom. This is the light shining in a dark place that you need to pay attention to. Let others indulge their imagination with an imaginary "church of the future." Let the children of this world dream of some "coming man" who is to understand everything and set everything right. They are only bringing on themselves bitter disappointment. They will awake to find their visions baseless and empty as a dream. It is to people such as these that the prophet's words may be well applied: *Behold, all ye that kindle a fire, that compass yourselves about with sparks: walk in the light of your fire, and in the sparks that ye have kindled. This shall ye have of mine hand; ye shall lie down in sorrow* (Isaiah 50:11).

But let your eyes look forward to the day of Christ's second advent. That is the only day when every abuse will be rectified and every corruption and source of sorrow completely purged away. While waiting for that day, let us each work on and serve our generation. Do not be idle, as if nothing can be done to check evil, but neither be disheartened because we do not yet see all things put under our Lord. After all, the night is almost over and the day is at hand. Let us wait, I say, on the Lord.

And if these things are true, you will not wonder why we warn you to beware of all leanings toward the Church of Rome. Surely, when the mind of God about idolatry is so plainly revealed to us in His Word, it seems the height of foolish infatuation in anyone to join a church so steeped in idolatries as the Church of Rome. To enter into communion with her when God is saying, *Come out of her, my people, that ye be not partakers of her sins, and that ye receive not of her plagues* (Revelation 18:4); to seek her when the Lord is warning us to leave her; to become her subjects when the Lord's voice is crying, "Escape for thy life, *flee from the wrath to come*" is mental blindness. It is a blindness like that of him who, though forewarned, goes on board a sinking ship, a blindness that would be almost incredible if our own eyes did not see examples of it continually.

We must all be on our guard. We must take nothing for granted. We must not hastily suppose that we are too wise to be ensnared and say like Hazael, *Is thy servant a dog, that he should do this great thing?* (2 Kings 8:13). We who preach must cry aloud and not allow a false tenderness to make us keep silent about the heresies of the day. You who hear must be ready with the truth and store in your minds clear prophetic views of the end to which all idol worshippers must come. Let us all try to grasp the reality that the latter ends of the world are upon us and that the abolition of all idolatry is hastening on. Is this the time for someone to move nearer to Rome? Is it not rather a time to pull further back and stand clear to avoid being caught in her downfall? Is this a time to excuse and disguise Rome's multiple corruptions and refuse to see the reality of her sins? Instead, we ought to especially guard against a Roman Catholic tendency in religion, be especially careful to not allow any treason against our Lord Christ, and be especially ready to protest against unscriptural worship of every description. Remember that the destruction of all idolatry is certain, and remembering that, beware the Church of Rome.

Let me conclude by giving you some safeguards and protections for your souls. You live in a time when the Church of Rome is walking among us with renewed strength and loudly boasting that she will soon win back the ground that she has lost. False doctrines of every kind are continually set before you in the most subtle and misleading forms, so it cannot be thought untimely if I offer you some practical safeguards against idolatry. What it is, where it comes from, where it is, what will end it – all this you have heard. Let me point out how you may keep safe from it and I will say no more.

Arm yourselves with a thorough knowledge of the Word of God. Read it more diligently than ever. Become familiar with every part of it. Let it dwell in you richly. Beware of anything which would make you give less time and less heart to the scrutiny of its sacred pages. The Bible is the sword of the Spirit; let it never be laid aside. The Bible is the true lantern for a dark and cloudy time; beware of traveling without its light.

If we knew the secret history of those deplorable defections from our church to that of Rome, I strongly suspect that in almost every case one of the most important steps in the downward road would be a neglected Bible – more attention to forms, sacraments, daily services, early Christianity, and so forth, and diminished attention to the written Word of God. The Bible is the King's highway. Once you leave that for any other path, however beautiful and old and frequented it may seem, you should not be surprised if you end up worshipping images and relics.

Arm yourselves with a godly jealousy about even the smallest part of the gospel. Do not approve even the slightest attempt to keep back any jot or tittle of it or to throw any part of it into the shade by exalting subordinate matters in religion. It seemed a small thing when Peter stopped eating with the gentiles, but Paul tells the Galatians, *I withstood him to the face, because he was to be blamed* (Galatians 2:11). Do not count anything little that concerns your soul. Be very particular about whom you listen to, where you go, and what you do in all the matters of your own particular worship. Do not care if you are accused of being squeamish or of having excessively high principles. You live in days when great principles are involved in little acts, and things in religion, which years ago were utterly indifferent, are now by circumstances rendered indifferent no longer. Be careful not to tamper with anything of a Romanizing tendency; it is foolish to play with fire. I believe that many who left our church for the Church of Rome began by thinking there was no great in harm in attaching just a little more importance to certain outward things than they once did. But once launched on the downward course, they went on from one thing to another. They provoked God and He left them to themselves. They tempted the devil and he came to them. They started with trifles, as many foolishly call them, and they have ended with downright idolatry.

And last of all, arm yourselves above all with clear, sound views of our Lord Jesus Christ and of the salvation that is in Him. He is the image of the invisible God – the express image of His person, and when truly known, He is the true preservative against all idolatry. Build yourselves deep down on the strong foundation of His finished work upon the cross. Settle this firmly in your mind: Christ Jesus has done everything needed in order to present you without spot before the throne of God, and that simple, childlike faith on your part is the only thing required to give you an entire interest in the work of Christ. And that having this faith, you are completely justified in the sight of God. You will not be more justified if you live to the age of Methuselah and do the works of the apostle Paul, and you can add nothing to that complete justification by any acts, deeds, works, performances, fastings, prayers, alms, attendance on ordinances, or anything else of your own.

And keep up, I beg you, continual communion with the person of the Lord Jesus. Abide in Him daily, feed on Him daily, look to Him daily, lean on Him daily, live upon Him daily, draw from His fullness daily. Do this and the idea of other mediators, other comforters, other intercessors will seem utterly absurd. "What need is there?" You will reply, "I have Christ, and in Him I have all."

Let the Lord Christ have His rightful place in your heart and all other things in your religion will soon fall into their right places. Church, ministers, sacraments, ordinances – all will go down and take second place.

Unless Christ sits as High Priest and King upon the throne of your heart, that little kingdom within will be in perpetual confusion. But let Him be all in all there, and I will have no fear for you. Before Him every idol, every Dagon, will fall.

Chapter 5

Scattered Israel to Be Gathered

Hear the word of the Lord, *O ye nations, and declare it in the isles afar off, and say, He that scattered Israel will gather him, and keep him, as a shepherd doth his flock.* (Jeremiah 31:10)

The text which heads this page is remarkably full and comprehensive. It contains both history and prophecy. It speaks of the scattering of Israel; this is history. It speaks of the gathering of Israel; this is prophecy. It demands the attention of both the Jew and the gentile. To the Jew it holds out a hope: Israel, it says, will be gathered. On the gentile it lays a command: *Hear the word of the* Lord, it says, *O ye nations, and declare it in the isles afar off, and say, He that scattered Israel will gather him.*

The whole body of gentile Christendom is specially addressed in this text. There is no evading this conclusion with any fair interpretation of Scripture. We ourselves are among the *nations* to whom Jeremiah speaks. To us is delegated a portion of the duty which he here sets forth. The text is the Lord's voice to all the churches of Christ among the gentiles. It is a voice to the churches of England, Scotland, and Ireland. It is a voice to the churches of Germany, Switzerland, Sweden, Holland, Denmark, and America. It is a voice to all Christendom. And what does the voice say? It commands us to proclaim far and wide the will of God concerning the Jewish nation. It tells us to remind one another of God's past and future dealings with Israel. *He that scattered Israel will gather him.*

I ask for your serious attention while I try to explain the Jewish subject to you in a connected and condensed form. I propose to show you from Scripture the past, the present, and the future of Israel. I know few texts in the Bible which contain such a complete summary of the subject as this one from Jeremiah. I will attempt to unfold this text.

I ask you not to dismiss the subject as speculative, fanciful, or unprofitable. The world is growing old; the last days are come upon us. The foundations of the earth are out of order. The ancient institutions of society are wearing out and falling to pieces. The end of all things is at hand. Surely it is fitting for a wise person, at a time like this, to turn to the pages of prophecy and inquire what is yet to come. At a time like this the declarations of God concerning His people Israel ought to be carefully weighed and examined. *Till the time of the end,* says Daniel, *the wise shall understand* (Daniel 12:9-10).

There are four points I want to keep our attention on as we consider the words from our text in Jeremiah:

1. The meaning of the word *Israel,* both here and elsewhere in Scripture

2. The present condition of Israel

3. The future prospects for Israel

4. The duty which gentile churches owe to Israel

The meaning of the word Israel

The definition of terms is of first importance in theology. Unless we explain the meaning of the words we use in our religious statements, our arguments are often wasted, and we seem like men beating the air.

The word *Israel* is used nearly seven hundred times in the Bible. I can only discover three senses in which it is used. First, it is one of the names of Jacob, the father of the twelve tribes, a name specially given to him by God. Second, it is a name given to the ten tribes which separated from Judah and Benjamin in the days of Rehoboam and became a distinct kingdom. This kingdom is often called Israel in contradistinction to the kingdom of Judah. And third, it is a name given to the whole Jewish nation, to all members of the twelve tribes which sprung from Jacob and were brought out of Egypt into the land of Canaan. This is by far the most common use of the word in the Bible. It is the only signification in which I can find the word *Israel* used throughout the whole New Testament. It is the same in which the word is used in the text which I am considering this day. That Israel, which God has scattered and will yet gather again, is the whole Jewish nation.

Now, why do I dwell upon this point? To some it may appear a mere waste of time and words to say so much about it. The things I have been saying sound to them like truisms. That Israel means Israel is a matter on which they never felt a doubt. If this is the mind of any of you, I am thankful for it. But unhappily there are many Christians who do not see the subject with your eyes, and for their sakes I must dwell on this point a little longer.

For many centuries there has prevailed in the churches of Christ a strange and, to my mind, an unjustified way of dealing with this word *Israel*. It has been interpreted in many passages of the Psalms and Prophets as if it meant nothing more than Christian believers. Have promises been held out to Israel? We have been told continually that they are addressed to gentile saints. Have glorious things been described as laid up in store for Israel? We have been incessantly told that they describe the victories and triumphs of the gospel in Christian churches. There are too many proofs of these things to require quotation. You cannot read most commentaries and popular hymns without seeing this system of interpretation. I have protested against that system for a long time and I hope I will protest as long as I live.

I do not deny that Israel was a distinctive people and that God's relationship with Israel was also meant to be a type of His relationship with His believing people all over the world.

I do not forget that it is written, *As in water face answereth to face, so the heart of man to man* (Proverbs 27:19), and that whatever spiritual truths are taught in prophecy concerning Israelite hearts are also applicable to the hearts of gentiles.

It should be most distinctly understood that God's dealings with individual Jews and gentiles are precisely one and the same. Without repentance, faith in Christ, and holiness of heart, no individual Jew or gentile will ever be saved.

What I protest is the habit of allegorizing plain sayings of the Word of God concerning the future history of the nation of Israel, and explaining away the fullness of their contents in order to accommodate them to the gentile church. I believe the habit is unwarranted by anything in Scripture and draws after it a long train of evil consequences.

Where, I ask, in the whole New Testament do we find any plain authority for applying the word *Israel* to anyone but the nation of Israel? I can find none. On the contrary, I observe that when the apostle Paul quotes Old Testament prophecies about the privileges of the gentiles in gospel times, he is careful to quote texts which specially mention the gentiles by name. The fifteenth chapter of the epistle to the Romans is a striking illustration of what I mean. We are often told in the New Testament that under the gospel, believing gentiles are fellow heirs and partakers of the same hope with believing Jews (Ephesians 3:6). But I cannot see anywhere at all that believing gentiles may be called Israelites.

We can see in many Christian writers a loose system of interpreting the language of the Psalms and Prophets and an exaggerated expectation of universal conversion of the world by the preaching of the gospel. To what can we attribute this? To nothing so much, I believe, as to the habit of inaccurately interpreting the word *Israel* and to the consequent application of promises to the gentile churches, with which they have nothing to do. The least errors in theology always bear fruit. No one ever accepts an incorrect principle of interpreting Scripture without that principle entailing awkward consequences and coloring the whole tone of his religion.

I will leave this part of my subject now, but I am sure that its importance cannot be overrated. In fact, a right understanding of it lies at the very root of the whole Jewish subject and of the prophecies concerning the Jews. The duty which Christians owe to Israel as a nation will never be clearly understood until Christians clearly see the place that Israel occupies in Scripture.

Before going any further, I will ask one plain, practical question.

I ask you to consider calmly what meaning you give to such words as *Israel, Jacob,* and the like when you meet with them in the Psalms and prophecies of the Old Testament. We live in a day when there are many Bible readers. There are many who search the Scriptures regularly and read through the Psalms and the Prophets once, if not twice, every year they live. Of course, you attach some meaning to the words I have just referred to. You place some sense upon them. Now what is that sense? What is that meaning? Consider carefully that it is the right one.

Accept a friendly exhortation this day. Cling to the literal sense of Bible words and beware of departing from it except in cases of absolute necessity. Be wary of that system of allegorizing, spiritualizing, and accommodating which the school of Origen first brought in and which has found such an unfortunate degree of favor in the church. In reading the authorized version of the English Bible, do not put too much confidence in the headings of pages and tables of contents at beginnings of chapters, which I consider a most unhappy accompaniment to that admirable translation. Remember that those headings and tables of contents were invented by uninspired hands. In reading the Prophets, they are sometimes not helps but real hindrances, and are less likely to assist a reader than to lead him astray. When reading the Psalms and the Prophets, fix it in your mind that Israel means Israel and Zion means Zion and Jerusalem means Jerusalem. And finally, whatever edification you derive from applying to your own soul the words which God addresses to His ancient people, never lose sight of the primary sense of the text.

The present condition of Israel

The expression used by Jeremiah describes exactly the state in which the Jews are at this day and have been for almost two thousand years. They are a scattered people. The armies of Assyria, Babylon, and Rome have, one after another, swept over the land of Israel and carried its inhabitants into captivity. Few, if any, of the ten tribes appear to have returned from the Assyrian captivity. Less than fifty thousand of Judah and

Benjamin came back from the captivity of Babylon. From the last and worst captivity, when the temple was burned and Jerusalem destroyed, there has been no return at all.[35] For centuries Israel has been dispersed over the four quarters of the globe. Like the wreck of some considerable ship, the Jews have been tossed to and fro on all waters and stranded in broken pieces on every shore.

But though Israel has been scattered, Israel has not been destroyed. For almost two thousand years the Jews have continued as a separate people, without a king, without a land, without a territory, but never lost, never absorbed among other nations. They have often been trampled underfoot but never shaken from the faith of their fathers. They have often been persecuted but never destroyed. At this very moment they are as distinct and peculiar a people as any people upon earth, an unanswerable argument in the way of the infidel, a puzzling difficulty in the way of politicians, a standing lesson to all the world. Romans, Danes, Saxons, Normans, Belgians, French, and Germans have all in turn settled on English soil. All have in turn lost their national distinctiveness. All have in turn become part and parcel of the English nation after the lapse of a few hundred years. But it has never been so with the Jews. Dispersed as they are, there is a principle of cohesion among them which no circumstances have been able to melt. Scattered as they are, there is a national vitality among them which is stronger than that of any nation on earth. Go where you will, you always find them. Settle where you please, in hot countries or in cold, you will find Jews. But go where you will and settle where you please, this wonderful people is always the same. Scattered as they are, few in number compared to those among whom they live, the Jews are always the Jews. Three thousand years ago Balaam said, *The people shall dwell alone, and shall not be reckoned among the nations* (Numbers 23:9). Two thousand years ago our Lord said, *This generation shall not pass away, till all be fulfilled* (Luke 21:32). We see these words made good before our eyes.

But by whose hands was this scattering of Israel brought about? The text before us today expressly declares that it was the hand of God. It was not the armies of Tiglath-Pileser or Shalmaneser or Nebuchadnezzar or Titus. They were only instruments in the hand of a far higher power. It

---

35 This was written in the nineteenth century, before the founding of the state of Israel.

was the God who orders all things in heaven and earth who dispersed the twelve tribes over the face of the earth. It was the same God who brought Israel out of Egypt with a high hand and mighty arm and planted them in Canaan who plucked them up by the roots and made them *wanderers among the nations* (Hosea 9:17).

Why did God send this heavy judgment upon Israel? To what are we to attribute this extraordinary dispersion of a people who were so highly favored? The question is a very useful one. Let us consider the answer.

The Jews are a scattered people because of their many sins. Their hardness and obstinacy, their impenitence and unbelief, their abuse of privileges and neglect of gifts, their rejection of prophets and messengers from heaven, and finally their refusal to receive the Lord Jesus Christ, the King's own Son, were the things which called down God's wrath upon them. These were the causes of their present dispersion. The vine which was brought out of Egypt bore wild grapes. The husbandman to whom the vineyard was rented out did not give the fruit he owed to the Lord of the vineyard. The people that were brought out of the house of bondage rebelled against Him by whom they were set free. As a result, the wrath of God rose until there was no remedy. He says, *You only have I known of all the families of the earth: therefore I will punish you for all your iniquities* (Amos 3:2). They *killed the Lord Jesus, and their own prophets, and have persecuted us; and they please not God, and are contrary to all men: forbidding us to speak to the Gentiles that they might be saved, to fill up their sins alway: for the wrath is come upon them to the uttermost* (1 Thessalonians 2:15-16).

Israel was scattered to be a perpetual warning to the gentile churches of Christ. The Jews are God's beacon or pillar of salt to all Christendom and a silent standing lesson that all who profess to know God ought never to forget. They proclaim to all Christians God's hatred of spiritual pride and self-righteousness, God's high displeasure with those who exalt the traditions of men and depart from the Word, and God's hatred of formalism and ceremonialism. If you want to know how much God hates these things, you need only to look at the present condition of the Jews. For eighteen hundred years God has held them up before the eyes of the world and written His abhorrence of their sins in letters that all may read.

I cannot leave this part of my subject without asking you to learn a practical lesson from the scattering of Israel. I urge you to remember the causes which led to their dispersion and to be careful to not get even close to their peculiar sins. I am sure the warning is needed in these latter days. I am sure that the opinions which are boldly introduced and openly maintained by many religious teachers in all churches of Christendom call loudly on all Christians to be on their guard. It is with good reason that our Lord said, *Take heed and beware of the leaven of the Pharisees and of the Sadducees* (Matthew 16:6). Look to your own heart. Beware of dabbling with false doctrines. Churches are never safe unless their members know their individual responsibility. Let us each look to ourselves and take care of our own souls. The same God lives who scattered Israel because of Israel's sins. And what does He say to the churches of Christ today? He says, *Be not highminded, but fear: For if God spared not the natural branches, take heed lest he also spare not thee* (Romans 11:20-21).

The future prospects for Israel

In taking up this branch of my subject, I feel that I am entering into the region of unfulfilled prophecy. I desire to do so with all reverence and with a deep sense of the many difficulties surrounding this department of theology and the many diversities of opinion that prevail upon it. But the servant of God must call no man master on earth. Truth is never likely to be attained unless all ministers of Christ speak their opinions fully, freely, and unreservedly, and give men an opportunity to weigh what they teach.

The difficulties surrounding many parts of unfulfilled prophecy are great, but two points stand out to me as plainly as if written by a sunbeam. One of these points is that the second personal advent of our Lord Jesus Christ will happen before the millennium. The other is the future literal gathering of the Jewish nation and their restoration to their own land. I do not tell anyone that these two truths are essential to salvation and that you cannot be saved unless you see them as I do.

But I do tell people that these truths appear to me distinctly recorded in Holy Scripture, and that the denial of them is as astonishing and incomprehensible to my mind as the denial of the divinity of Christ.

Now what does our text say about the future prospects of the Jews? What can we expect? It says, *He that scattered Israel will gather him.* That gathering is an event which plainly is yet to come. It could not apply in any sense to the ten tribes of Israel. They have never been gathered in any way. Their scattering has never come to an end. It cannot be applied to the return of the remnant of Judah and Benjamin from the Babylon captivity. The language of the text makes such an application impossible. The text is addressed to the gentiles: *ye nations.* The declaration they are commanded to make is *in the isles afar off.* In the days of the Babylon captivity, the nations of the earth knew nothing of the word of the Lord. They were sunk in darkness and had not even heard the Lord's name. If Jeremiah had told them to proclaim the return of the Jews from Babylon under such circumstances, it would have been useless and absurd. There is but one fair and legitimate interpretation of the promise of the text. The event it declares is still future. The gathering spoken of is a gathering which is yet to come.

I believe that the interpretation I have just given is entirely in harmony with many other plain prophecies of Scripture. I do not have time to quote even a tenth of the texts that teach the same truth. Out of the sixteen Prophets of the Old Testament, there are at least ten in which the gathering and restoration of the Jews in the latter days are expressly mentioned. From each of these ten I will take one testimony. I say "one" deliberately because I am anxious not to overload the subject with evidence. I would only remind you that the texts I am about to quote are only a small portion of the evidence that might be brought forward.

1. Hear what Isaiah says: *It shall come to pass in that day, that the Lord shall set his hand again the second time to recover the remnant of his people, which shall be left, from Assyria, and from Egypt, and from Pathros, and from Cush, and from Elam, and from Shinar, and from Hamath, and from the islands of the sea. And he shall set up an ensign for the nations, and shall assemble the outcasts of Israel, and gather*

together the dispersed of Judah from the four corners of the earth (Isaiah 11:11-12).

2. Hear what Ezekiel says: *Thus saith the Lord God; Behold, I will take the children of Israel from among the heathen, whither they be gone, and will gather them on every side, and bring them into their own land* (Ezekiel 37:21).

3. Hear what Hosea says: *Then shall the children of Judah and the children of Israel be gathered together, and appoint themselves one head, and they shall come up out of the land: for great shall be the day of Jezreel. For the children of Israel shall abide many days without a king, and without a prince, and without a sacrifice, and without an image, and without an ephod, and without teraphim: afterward shall the children of Israel return, and seek the Lord their God, and David their king; and shall fear the Lord and his goodness in the latter days* (Hosea 1:11; 3:4-5).

4. Hear what Joel says: *But Judah shall dwell for ever, and Jerusalem from generation to generation* (Joel 3:20).

5. Hear what Amos says: *And I will bring again the captivity of my people of Israel, and they shall build the waste cities, and inhabit them; and they shall plant vineyards, and drink the wine thereof; they shall also make gardens, and eat the fruit of them. And I will plant them upon their land, and they shall no more be pulled up out of their land which I have given them, saith the Lord thy God* (Amos 9:14-15).

6. Hear what Obadiah says: *But upon mount Zion shall be deliverance, and there shall be holiness; and the house of Jacob shall possess their possessions* (Obadiah 1:17).

7. Hear what Micah says: *In that day, saith the Lord, will I assemble her that halteth, and I will gather her that is driven out, and her that I have afflicted; and I will make her that halted a remnant, and her that was cast far off a strong*

nation: and the Lord shall reign over them in mount Zion from henceforth, even for ever* (Micah 4:6-7).

8. Hear what Zephaniah says: *Sing, O daughter of Zion; shout, O Israel; be glad and rejoice with all the heart, O daughter of Jerusalem. The Lord hath taken away thy judgments, he hath cast out thine enemy: the king of Israel, even the Lord, is in the midst of thee: thou shalt not see evil any more. In that day it shall be said to Jerusalem, Fear thou not: and to Zion, Let not thine hands be slack. The Lord thy God in the midst of thee is mighty; he will save, he will rejoice over thee with joy; he will rest in his love, he will joy over thee with singing. I will gather them that are sorrowful for the solemn assembly, who are of thee, to whom the reproach of it was a burden. Behold, at that time I will undo all that afflict thee: and I will save her that halteth, and gather her that was driven out; and I will get them praise and fame in every land where they have been put to shame. At that time will I bring you again, even in the time that I gather you: for I will make you a name and a praise among all people of the earth, when I turn back your captivity before your eyes, saith the Lord* (Zephaniah 3:14-20).

9. Hear what Zechariah says: *And I will strengthen the house of Judah, and I will save the house of Joseph, and I will bring them again to place them; for I have mercy upon them: and they shall be as though I had not cast them off: for I am the Lord their God, and will hear them. And they of Ephraim shall be like a mighty man, and their heart shall rejoice as through wine: yea, their children shall see it, and be glad; their heart shall rejoice in the Lord. I will hiss for them, and gather them; for I have redeemed them: and they shall increase as they have increased. And I will sow them among the people: and they shall remember me in far countries; and they shall live with their children, and turn again. I will bring them again also out of the land of Egypt, and gather them out of Assyria; and I will bring them into the land of*

Gilead and Lebanon; and place shall not be found for them (Zechariah 10:6-10).

10. Hear, lastly, what Jeremiah says: *For, lo, the days come, saith the* Lord, *that I will bring again the captivity of my people Israel and Judah, saith the* Lord: *and I will cause them to return to the land that I gave to their fathers, and they shall possess it. For I am with thee, saith the* Lord, *to save thee: though I make a full end of all nations whither I have scattered thee, yet I will not make a full end of thee: but I will correct thee in measure, and will not leave thee altogether unpunished* (Jeremiah 30:3, 11).

I place these texts before you without note or comment. I only hope that you will weigh and examine them and read carefully the several chapters from which they are taken. I believe there is one common remark that applies to them all: they all point to a time which is yet future. They all predict the final gathering of the Jewish nation from the four quarters of the globe and the restoration to their own land.

Much more could be said about this subject, but I am resolved, however, not to encumber it by bringing in topics of comparatively subordinate importance. I will not complicate it by elaborating on the manner in which Israel will be gathered and the particular events which will accompany the gathering. I might show you by scriptural evidence that the Jews will probably first be gathered in an unconverted state, though humbled, and will afterward, through much tribulation, be taught to look to Him whom they have pierced. I might speak of the future glory of Jerusalem after the Jews are restored, and the last siege, described by Zechariah and our Lord Jesus Christ, which it will endure. But I refrain. I will not travel beyond the bounds of my text. I think it better to present its weighty promise to you in its naked simplicity. Israel scattered will yet be gathered. This is the future hope and prospect of the Jews.

Now is there anything contrary to this gathering found in the New Testament? I cannot find a single word. Not only do I find nothing contrary to this, but also I do find a chapter in the epistle to the Romans where an inspired apostle fully discusses the subject. And there he speaks of Israel being once more *received* into God's favor, *grafted in,* and *saved* (see Romans 11:15-32).

Is there anything impossible in this gathering of Israel? Who talks of impossibilities? If an unbeliever, let him explain the present condition and past history of Israel if he can. And when he has solved that mighty problem, we may listen to him. If a Christian, let him think again before he talks of anything being impossible with God. Let him read the vision of the dry bones in Ezekiel and mark to whom that vision applies. Let him look to his own conversion and resurrection from the death of trespasses and sins and then recall the unworthy thought that anything is too hard for the Lord.

> Reasoning from analogy, I can see no ground for refusing to believe that God may still do wonderful things for the Jewish people.

Is there anything inconsistent with God's former dealings in the gathering of Israel? Is there any extravagance in expecting such an event? Why should we say so? Reasoning from analogy, I can see no ground for refusing to believe that God may still do wonderful things for the Jewish people. It would not be more marvelous to see them gathered once more into Palestine than it was to see them brought from Egypt into the promised land. What God has done once, He may certainly do again.

Is there anything improbable in the gathering of Israel? Oh, we are poor judges of probabilities! God's ways of carrying into effect His own purposes are not to be judged by man's standard or measured by the plumb line of what man calls probable. In the day when the children of Israel went out from Egypt, would anyone have said it was probable that such a nation of serfs would produce a book that would turn the world upside down? Yet that nation has done it; from that nation has come the Bible. Four thousand years ago would anyone have said it was probable that God's Son would come to earth and suffer in the flesh on a cross before He came to earth in glory to reign? But that is what happened. Christ has lived and Christ has suffered and Christ has died. Away with this talk about improbabilities! The ways of God are not our ways.

Finally, is there anything fanatical or overly enthusiastic in this expectation that Israel will be gathered? Why should you say so? Your own eyes tell you that the present order of things will never convert the world. There is not a church or a parish or a congregation where the converted are more than a little flock. There is not a faithful minister on earth, and never has been, who has ever seen more than the "taking out of a people" to serve Christ (Acts 15:14). A change must come before the earth will be filled with the knowledge of the Lord. A new order of teachers must be raised up and a new dispensation ushered in. These teachers, I firmly believe, will be converted Jews. And then will be seen the fulfillment of the remarkable words, *If the casting away of them be the reconciling of the world, what shall the receiving of them be, but life from the dead?* (Romans 11:15).

I will not stay any longer on this branch of my subject. I leave it with one general remark, which may sound to some readers like a bald truism. Whether it be a truism or not, I believe the remark to be of vital importance, and I heartily wish that it was more deeply impressed on all our minds.

Settle it firmly in your mind that when God says a thing will be done we ought to believe it. We have no right to begin talking of probable and improbable, likely and unlikely, possible and impossible, reasonable and unreasonable. What is this but veiled skepticism and unbelief in disguise? What has the Lord said? What has He spoken? What do the Scriptures say? What is written in the Word? These are the only questions we have a right to ask, and when the answer to them is plain, we have nothing to do but believe. Our reason may rebel. Our preconceived ideas of what God ought to do may receive a rude shock. Our private systems of prophetic interpretation may be shattered to pieces. Our secret prejudices may be grievously offended. But what are we to do? We must abide by Scripture or be of all men most miserable. At any cost let us cling to the Word. *Let God be true, but every man a liar* (Romans 3:4).

In all matters of unfulfilled prophecy, I desire to fall back on this principle. I see many things I cannot explain. I find many difficulties I cannot solve. But I dare not give up my principle. I am determined to believe everything that God says. I know it will all prove true at the last day. I read that He says in the text before us this day, *He that scattered*

Israel will gather him. Whatever the difficulties, it must be true. I steadfastly believe that Israel will be gathered.

The duty which gentile churches owe to Israel

In touching on this point, I do not want you for a moment to suppose that the future gathering of Israel depends on anything that man can do. God's counsels and purposes are independent of human strength. The sun will set tonight at its appointed hour, and neither queens, lords, nor commons, popes, presidents, nor emperors can hasten, prevent, or put off its setting. The tides of the sea will ebb and flow this week in their regular course, and no scientific decree nor engineering skill can interfere with their motion. And in the same way the promises of God concerning Israel will all be fulfilled in due season, whether we listen or not. When the times and seasons arrive, which God *hath put in his own power* (Acts 1:7), Israel will be gathered – and all the alliances and combinations of statesmen and all the persecution and unbelief of apostate churches will not be able to prevent it.

But since these things are coming, it would benefit us to be found doing the right things. It is our duty to seriously consider these questions: What manner of persons should we be and in what way can we testify to our full agreement with God's purposes for the Jews? Can we in no sense be fellow workers with God? Should we not remember that remarkable saying of Paul: *Through your mercy they also may obtain mercy* (Romans 11:31)? These are the questions to which I now desire to supply a brief, practical answer.

The first duty, then, for gentile Christians, is to *take a special interest in the spiritual condition of the Jewish nation* and to give their conversion a special place in our prayers. I deliberately say their spiritual condition. I leave alone their civil and political position. I speak, exclusively, of our duty to Jewish souls. I say that we owe them a special debt and that this debt ought to be carefully paid.

We prize our Bibles, and we are right to do so. A heaven without a sun would not be more blank than a world without a Bible. But do we ever consider that every page in that blessed Book was written under God's inspiration by Israelite hands? Remember that every chapter and verse you read in your Bible you owe under God to Israel. There is not a religious society that meets in London in the month of May[36] which is not constantly working with Israelite tools.

We prize the glorious gospel of the grace of God, and we are right to do so. A land without the gospel, like Tartary[37] and China, is nothing better than a moral wilderness. See the vast difference between Europe and America with the gospel, notwithstanding all their vices, and Africa and Asia without it. But do we ever think that the first preachers of that gospel were all Jews? The men who, at the cost of their lives, first carried from town to town the blessed tidings of Christ crucified were not gentiles. The first to take up the lamp of truth, which was passed from hand to hand until it reached our heathen forefathers, were all men of Israel.

We rejoice in Christ Jesus and glory in His person and work. It is good that we do! Without a living Savior and the blood of His atonement once made on the cross, we should indeed be miserable. But do we ever consider that when that Savior became a man, in order that as man's substitute He might live and suffer and die, He was born of a Jewish woman? Yes! Let that never be forgotten. When *God was manifest in the flesh* and was *born of a woman,* that woman was a virgin of the house of David. When the promised Savior took flesh and blood that He might bruise the serpent's head and redeem man, He did not take flesh and blood of any royal house among the gentiles but of one of the twelve tribes of Israel.

I know that these are ancient things. They have been often urged, often alleged, often pressed on the attention of the churches. I am not ashamed to bring them forward again. If there be such a thing as gratitude in the heart of man, it is the duty of all gentile Christians to take special interest in the work of doing good to the Jews.

I believe, furthermore, that it is a duty of all gentile Christians to be especially careful to *remove stumbling blocks from the way of Israel* and to see that they do nothing to disgust them with Christianity or hinder their conversion. This is a matter which is expressly mentioned in

---

36   Many religious groups and societies held their formal or annual meetings in London during the month of May.

37   *Tartary* was a term used to refer to a large region of Central Asia.

Scripture. There we find Isaiah bidding us, *Take up the stumblingblock out of the way of my* [God's] *people* (Isaiah 57:14). Truly the prophet might well speak of this. No man can look around the gentile churches and not see that he had cause.

What can we say of the glaring unholiness and neglect of God's Ten Commandments which prevail so widely in Christendom? What can we say of the open, unblushing idolatry which offends the eye in all Roman Catholic churches? What can we say of the widespread habit of Sabbath-breaking which is eating like a cancer into the heart of the Protestant churches? What can we say of the rationalistic method of interpreting Old Testament history that regards the histories of Abraham, Jacob, Joseph, and the like as so many myths or ingenious fables but not as narratives of facts which really took place, and which has crept so extensively into modern commentaries? What can we say of the traditional mode of interpreting Old Testament prophecies in which so many Christians indulge? This system appropriates all the blessings to the church of Christ and hands over all the bitter things to poor, despised Israel; interprets all prophecies about Christ's first advent literally and all prophecies about His second advent figuratively, requiring the Jew to believe the first to the letter, but refusing in turn to believe the second except in what is called, by a sad misnomer, a *spiritual* sense. What can we say of all these things, except that they are stumbling blocks – great stumbling blocks – in the way of the conversion of the Jews? What are they all but great barriers between the Jew and Christ, and barriers put up by Christian hands?

We must all do our part to help take these stumbling blocks away. Here at least all may help. Here every gentile Christian can aid the Jewish cause. The more pure and lovely we can make our holy faith, the more we are likely to recommend it to Israel. The more we can check the progress of the Roman apostasy and protest against its idolatries and corruptions, the more likely are the Jews to believe there is something in Christianity. The more we can promote the habit of interpreting all Scripture in its plain, literal sense, the more we are likely to remove prejudices in the minds of honest inquirers in Israel and to make them ready to hear what we have to say.

Finally, I believe it is a duty of all gentile Christians to *use special efforts to promote the conversion of the Jews*. I say "special efforts" advisedly. The Jews are a peculiar people, a special people, and must be approached in a peculiar way.

They are peculiar in their state of mind. They require an entirely different treatment from the heathen. Their objections are not the heathen's objections. Their difficulties are not the heathen's difficulties. They believe many things that the heathen have never heard of. They have a standard of right and wrong with which the heathen man is utterly unacquainted. Like the heathen they need to be converted. Like the heathen they need to be brought to Christ. But the lines of argument to be pursued with the Jew and the heathen are widely dissimilar. A faithful missionary who might do admirably well among the heathen might find it difficult to reason with a Jew.

They are peculiar in their position in the world. They will not be found all assembled together like the Africans at Sierra Leone or the Hindus or New Zealanders or Chinese. They are emphatically a scattered people, a few in one country and a few in another. An effort to reach them must aim at nothing short of sending missionaries in search of them all over the world.

Circumstances like these appear to me to point out clearly that nothing less than a special effort will ever enable Christians to discharge their debt to Israel. There must be a division of labor in the mission field. There must be a special concentration of preaching, praying, and loving interactions with the Jewish people, or the churches of the gentiles can never expect to do them much spiritual good. Without such special effort, the cause of Israel will inevitably be lost sight of in the cause of the whole heathen world. Without such special effort, I cannot see how the command of the text can be rightly obeyed.

This is the claim that the London Society for Promoting Christianity amongst the Jews[38] makes on English Christians in the present day for aid. It enables them to make a special effort on behalf of Israel. It

---

38 The London Society for Promoting Christianity amongst the Jews (now called the Church's Ministry among Jewish People) was an Anglican missionary society that worked both in England and around the world.

supplies them with an outlet for their sympathy and a faithful agency for sending the gospel to God's ancient people. It is in this light that I earnestly commend the Society for the support of all who love the Lord Jesus Christ in sincerity and desire to do good in the world.

I am quite aware that it is commonly said that the Society does nothing. Its results appear to some to be very small and insignificant. I think that those who make such an objection have probably never considered the very special character of the work which the Society does. Its field is necessarily a remarkably scattered one. Its agents are necessarily scattered widely apart one from another. The work that they do, by the very nature of things, makes far less show than the work of a united band of missionaries at Tinnevelly or Sierra Leone. Tried by any fair standard, the work of the London Society for Promoting Christianity amongst the Jews has no cause to fear inspection. Its agents are bearing a testimony in some places and awakening in Israel thought, reflection, and inquiry. In others they are gradually softening prejudices and helping Jews become willing to hold discussions or listen to gospel statements. In others they are calling out a people and leading them to the foot of the cross. What more do we see going on at home? What greater results than these can be found in any congregation on earth where the gospel is preached? And, after all, duties are ours, and results are God's.

As I conclude, I pray that God will impress on your minds the three following comments:

Remember the special blessing which God has promised to all who care for Israel. Whatever a sneering world may say, the Jews are a people *beloved for their fathers' sakes.* Of Jerusalem it is written, *They shall prosper that love thee* (Psalm 122:6). Of Israel it is written, *Blessed is he that blesseth thee, and cursed is he that curseth thee* (Numbers 24:9). These promises are not yet depleted. We see their fulfillment in the blessing granted to the Church of England since the day when the Jewish cause was first taken up. We see their fulfillment in the special honor which God has put from time to time on individual Christians who have labored especially for the Jewish cause. Charles Simeon, Edward Bickersteth, Robert M'Cheyne, Haldane Stewart, and Dr. Marsh are striking examples of what I mean. Do you desire God's special blessing? Then labor for the cause of Israel, and you will find it.

Never forget the close connection which Scripture reveals between the time of Israel's gathering and the time of Christ's second advent to the world. In one psalm it is expressly declares, *When the LORD shall build up Zion, he shall appear in his glory* (Psalm 102:16). Where is the true believer who does not long for that blessed day? Where is the true Christian who does not cry from the bottom of his heart, *Thy kingdom come*? All Christians should work and give and pray so that the gospel may have free course in Israel and be glorified. The time to favor Zion is closely bound up with the restitution of all things. Blessed is that work that when complete will usher in the second coming of the Lord!

Finally, make sure of your own salvation. Do not rest in mere head knowledge of prophetic subjects. Do not be content with intellectual soundness in the faith. Diligently make your own calling and election sure. Seek to know that your repentance and faith are genuine and true. Seek to feel that you are one with Christ and Christ is in you and that you are washed, sanctified, and justified. Then, whether the completion of God's promises to Israel be near or far away, your own portion will be sure. You will stand in your lot safely when the kingdoms of this world are passing away. You will meet Christ without fear when He comes the second time to Zion. You will join boldly in the song, *Blessed is he that cometh in the name of the Lord.* You will sit down with Abraham, Isaac, and Jacob in the kingdom of God, and go out no more.[39]

---

[39] The substance of this address was originally preached as the annual sermon on behalf of the London Society for Promoting Christianity amongst the Jews at the Rectory Church, Marylebone, in May 1858.

Chapter 6

The Reading Which Is Blessed

The Revelation of Jesus Christ, which God gave unto him, to shew unto his servants things which must shortly come to pass; and he sent and signified it by his angel unto his servant John: who bare record of the word of God, and of the testimony of Jesus Christ, and of all things that he saw. Blessed is he that readeth, and they that hear the words of this prophecy, and keep those things which are written therein: for the time is at hand. (Revelation 1:1-3)

We live in troubled and dangerous times. It has been a long time since there have been as many ideas and events in our world causing fear and anxiety as there are today.

We are always apt to exaggerate the importance of events that happen in our own day. I do not forget that. But I cannot retract what I have just written. I look around me at the things now going on in the church and in the world. I look ahead to what could be our future. And as I look, I feel that I am justified in speaking of our times as troubled and dangerous. I appeal to the judgment of all who observe the history of their own times. Is there not a cause?

There are three heavy judgments which God can send on a nation: the sword, the pestilence, and the famine. All three of these have fallen heavily upon our country within the last few years. The Irish famine, the Russian war, the cholera, and the cattle plague have left marks on this country which cannot be erased. Surely these signs of the times deserve special notice. They should make us say with Habakkuk, *I will stand upon my watch, and set me upon the tower, and will watch to see what he will say unto me* (Habakkuk 2:1). They should make us cry with Daniel, *O my Lord, what shall be the end of these things?* (Daniel 12:8).

But one thing, in any event, is clear, and that is the duty of Christians to search more diligently than ever the prophetic Scriptures. Do not be like the Jews at the first advent who were blind to the hand of God and the fulfillment of His purposes in all that was going on in the world. Let us instead remember that the word of prophecy is given to be *a light that shineth in a dark place, until the day dawn, and the day star arise* (2 Peter 1:19). Let us walk in that light. Let us search *what, or what manner of time the Spirit of Christ which was in them* [the prophets] *did signify, when it testified beforehand the sufferings of Christ, and the glory that should follow* (1 Peter 1:11). Let us compare prophecies fulfilled with prophecies unfulfilled and attempt to make the one illustrate the other. Let us strive, above all, to obtain clear views of the things we should be expecting, both in the church and the world, before the end comes and time will be no more.

With such feelings I now invite you to consider the verses of Scripture quoted at the beginning of this chapter. Those verses are the preface or opening words of the book of Revelation. May the blessing which is specially promised to the readers and hearers of that book be with all of you!

There are three points to which I desire to call your attention:

1. The general character of the book of Revelation
2. The arguments commonly used to deter men from studying the book of Revelation
3. Useful lessons that the book of Revelation teaches

The general character of the book of Revelation

The book of Revelation differs widely from any other book of the Old or

New Testament. In many respects, it is thoroughly unlike the rest of the Bible. There is a solemn and majestic peculiarity about it. It stands alone.

It is peculiar in the dignity with which it begins. The very first verse prepares the reader for something extraordinary, for a book even more directly from God, if possible, than one written under the plenary inspiration of the Holy Spirit. It reads: *The Revelation of Jesus Christ, which God gave unto him, to shew unto his servants things which must shortly come to pass; and he sent and signified it by his angel unto his servant John.*

It is peculiar in the subject matter it contains. It contains less doctrinal and practical Christianity, in proportion to its length, than any other book of the New Testament. With few exceptions, its pages are filled with prophecies. These prophecies are of the widest range, extending, it seems to me, from the time of John to the very end of the world. They embrace a vast number of events that are spread over the whole *times of the Gentiles* (Luke 21:24), and cover the mighty interval between the destruction of the first Jerusalem and the descent of the new Jerusalem from heaven. And these prophecies are of universal importance to all mankind, having reference not only to the condition and prospects of the believing church, but also of the unconverted world.

It is peculiar in the style and dress in which its subject matter is clothed. With the exception of the second and third chapters, the greater part of the book is composed of visions which the apostle John saw in the Spirit. In these visions the vast range of the church's history was revealed to him under emblems, figures, allegories, symbols, and representations. The meaning of the great majority of these symbols and emblems is not explained. The general characteristics of these visions are greatly alike. All are marked by a vastness, a grandeur, a majesty, a life, a force, a boldness, and a sublimity entirely unparalleled in any human writings. The door opening in heaven, the voice like a trumpet speaking, the crystal-like sea of glass, the seven seals, the seven trumpets, the seven vials, the four angels holding the four winds, the mighty angel whose right foot is on the sea and his left foot on the earth and who has a face like the sun, the woman clothed with the sun and the moon under her feet, the great red dragon who has seven heads and ten horns, the beast rising out of the sea, the mighty earthquake, the destruction of Babylon, the summoning of the fowls of heaven to the supper of the great God, the binding of Satan, the great white throne, the last judgment, the descent of the new Jerusalem from heaven, the description of the glorious city – who can read such things without being struck by them? Who can study them and not come to the conclusion that this is *written with the finger of God*?

This is the general character of the book of Revelation and of this book which you are emphatically told it is blessed to read. I will offer just two general remarks on the symbolic style in which the book of Revelation is composed and then move on.

The first is that you must not regard the use of symbolic language as entirely peculiar to the book of Revelation. You will find it in other parts of Scripture. The very emblems and figures of the Apocalypse (another name for the book of Revelation), whose meaning seems so obscure, are often employed by the Holy Spirit in the Old Testament. You read, for example, of four living creatures in the fourth chapter of Revelation. You also read of four in Ezekiel (Ezekiel 1:5). You read of horses in the vision of the four first seals. You read of horses also in the vision of Zechariah (Zechariah 6:2-3). You read of a sealed group in the seventh chapter. You read also of a sealed and marked people in the vision of Ezekiel (Ezekiel 9). You read of a plague of locusts under the fifth trumpet. You read of locusts also in the prophecy of Joel (Joel 2). You read of John eating the little book in the tenth chapter. You read also of Ezekiel eating the roll in his vision (Ezekiel 3). You read of olive trees and candlesticks in the vision of the two witnesses. You read of the same emblems in the prophecy of Zechariah (Zechariah 4). In the thirteenth chapter, you read of a beast having seven heads and ten horns. You read of a similar beast in the book of Daniel (Daniel 7). You read of a wondrous celestial city in the twenty-first chapter of Revelation, and you have the description of a city scarcely less mysterious, though different, at the end of Ezekiel (Ezekiel 40-48). These things are worthy of comment. They show us that we must not stumble on the symbols of Revelation as if they were altogether a new and strange thing. We must remember they are used in the Old Testament as well as here, though far more sparingly, in communicating the mind of God to man. The peculiarity of the Apocalypse is not so much the use of symbols and emblems as the profuse abundance of them.

My other remark is that a symbolic style of composition will always seem stranger to us than it does to Eastern nations.[40] Figures, parables, illustrations, and similitudes are infinitely better known in the countries around the Holy Land than they are in the West. The hieroglyphic inscriptions, for example, which abound in Egypt and elsewhere in the East, are nothing more than symbolic writings. At first sight these hieroglyphics seem uncouth, meaningless, dark, and obscure. To study them, the first step you must take is to become familiar with their appearance. Then you may hope to become acquainted with the key to their meaning. Ultimately, when you find that key, you will find these hieroglyphics to be full of interesting matter. It is much the same with the book of Revelation. It is a book of sacred hieroglyphics. Its very style is one to which our matter-of-fact Northern mind is utterly unaccustomed. Its visions seem doubly strange to us – strange because we are not familiar with such a mode of conveying our ideas, but stranger still because in many cases we have no clue as to their meaning. Our first step must be to read and study them often, so we become familiar with their outward garb – with the style of composition in which they are clothed. If we study in a prayerful spirit, we may hope that the meaning of their inward contents will gradually be made plainer to our minds.

> If we study in a prayerful spirit, we may hope that the meaning of their inward contents will gradually be made plainer to our minds.

---

40 "The Symbolical or Hieroglyphical character is an art of communicating the conceptions of the mind by visible figures, which ... excite in others the same conceptions." – Charles Daubuz in *A Perpetual Commentary on the Revelation of St. John*, 1720.
"The Hieroglyphical characters are like all kinds of animals and members of men, and working tools, especially those of carpenters. For their writing does not show the discourse about the subject matter by the composition of syllables, but by the emphasis of the figures." – Diodorus Siculus, quoted by Daubuz.
"From this way of writing arose a symbolical way of speaking too; the symbolical characters, which they were so conversant with, furnishing them continually with metaphors and other tropes, first in their mysterious or religious speeches and from them easily passing on to the vulgar matters. Which kind of speech set up the priests and wiser sort of men above the level of the vulgar, because such a figurative and florid kind of speech and notions seemed to add great beauty to their thoughts and distinguished that of wise men from the plain style of the rest. Thence it comes that most of the Oriental languages, especially that of the poets, affect this way." – Daubuz.

One thing we need to remember and fix in our minds when reading the visions of the Apocalypse is that whether we understand little or much, every vision in the book has a real, definite meaning.

The time is short. We are quickly moving toward a day when every page will be unfolded and unsealed. Every knot will be untied. Every hard question will be answered. Then will we see that the book of Revelation, like every other part of the inspired volume, was all *very good*.

Then will we find that the blessing pronounced on its students was not given in vain, and that those readers whom God blesses are blessed indeed.

The arguments commonly used to deter men from studying the book of Revelation

There have always been "good" men who have belittled the study of Revelation as unprofitable. They have spoken of it as a book too dark and mysterious for use. They have told men to respect it as inspired, but to not touch it. Reverence it at a distance, as part of the Bible, but do not come near it or handle its contents. To this prejudice we probably owe the unfortunate omission of the book from the daily calendar of lessons in the liturgy of the Church of England. It is regrettable that in the last arrangement of that calendar the apocryphal story of Bel and the Dragon was thrust in and the Revelation of John the Divine was shut out. Room was made for an entirely uninspired composition, but no place was found for a book to the reading of which a special blessing is promised. Truly we may say in this case, *Great men are not always wise: neither do the aged understand judgment* (Job 32:9).[41]

When you see that such prejudices have existed against the study of the book of Revelation among good men, you will not be surprised that the children of the world have gone further. Men, more witty than wise, have launched sharp sayings, jests, and jibes at its students. They have not been ashamed to find a target for witticism in its solemn and

---

[41] It is a curious fact that the Fourth Council of Toledo, held about the year AD 640, made the following decree: "Because there are many that do not receive the book of Apocalypse as authentic, and scorn to read it in the Church of God, if any one for the future shall refuse to receive it, or to read it in the Church, in the time of Mass, from Easter to Whitsuntide, he shall be excommunicated." – Drue Cressener in *A Demonstration of the First Principles of Protestant Applications of the Apocalypse*, 1690.

mysterious visions. Even a man like Scaliger[42] declared that one of Calvin's wisest acts was his abstaining from writing a commentary on the book. Dr. South, a clever writer, though an unsound theologian, said that the study of Revelation either "found a man mad or made him so."

But is there any value in the objections commonly made to the study of Revelation? Let us weigh them in the balances. To my own mind they appear neither as serious nor as unanswerable as is commonly supposed.

One class of objectors dislikes the book because it seems to point to a coming state in the world, which to their minds is monstrous, incredible, and improbable.

That God should send plagues and judgments upon the nations of the earth because of their sins against Him – that the kings of the earth, and the great men, and the captains, and the rich, and the mighty, and the bound, and the free should really flee to hide themselves from the wrath of the Lamb – that the kingdoms of this world should really become the kingdoms of our God and of His Christ – that the saints of the Lord Jesus should forever reign upon the earth and everything that defiles will be cast out – all this is to their minds almost absurd. "It is contrary to common sense," they tell us. "It is a mark of a weak mind to believe it. It is extravagance. It is raving. It is enthusiasm. It is going back to the ranting of Fifth Monarchy Men[43] in the Commonwealth. It cannot be. We cannot show them the details of the way in which all these things will come to pass. They will not believe them. A book from which we draw such strange, fanatical opinions can never be a profitable one to study."

I boldly answer these objectors. They would do well to remember that the great and important events yet to come, to which Revelation points, are no more unimaginable than many which have already taken place in the world. The destruction of the old world by the flood, the wasting of Babylon, Nineveh, Tyre, and Egypt, the scattering of the Jews and their perpetual preservation, notwithstanding, as a separate people – all these were things utterly improbable at the time when they were prophesied. But we know that they all came to pass. And as

---

42 Joseph Justus Scaliger (1540–1609) was a French religious scholar.
43 Fifth Monarchy Men was an extreme Puritan sect in the 1600s that believed the time of the fifth monarchy (following the four mentioned in the book of Daniel) and thus Christ's rule on earth was near.

it has been in days gone by, so it will be in days to come. Men, in their pride, forget that in the eyes of an eternal God the movements of the nations of the earth are as the struggles of a few short-lived insects. In just a little time, despotic and constitutional governments, liberal and conservative parties – all will be swept away. God has said it, and with Him nothing is impossible.

As to the manner in which the great events predicted in Revelation will be brought about, we do not pretend to explain it. There are many things which we accept as facts but find it impossible to explain. We believe in the creation of all things out of nothing. We believe the fact of the incarnation. But who would dare to offer an explanation of any of these great mysteries? We have a right to regard unfulfilled prophecy in the same light. We believe the facts of the prophecies without knowing the mode of their fulfillment.

> The heart not taught by the Holy Spirit rebels against the idea of severe judgments against sin, a kingdom of Christ, and a reign of the saints.

I leave this first class of objectors here. I fear, in too many cases, that the secret spring of their arguments is the natural heart's dislike of spiritual things. The heart not taught by the Holy Spirit rebels against the idea of severe judgments against sin, a kingdom of Christ, and a reign of the saints. Why? The plain truth is that it is not so much the book of Revelation that such a heart objects to as it is the whole gospel of Christ and all the counsel of God.

Another class of objectors must next be noticed. These objectors deprecate the study of Revelation because of the wide differences which prevail in the interpretation of its contents and the notorious mistakes interpreters have made.

I do not for a moment pretend to deny the existence of these differences and mistakes. Some good men confidently tell us that the whole book is entirely unfulfilled. They demand an accomplishment of its visions so clear and unmistakable that there is no room left for doubt. Other good men assure us, with no less confidence, that the whole book is fulfilled with the exception of a small portion at the end. A third school of expositors maintains that Revelation is partly fulfilled and partly unfulfilled. As to the details of the book, the meaning and application of the several visions it contains, and the fulfillment of times and seasons – I would run out of time to recount the various interpretations that have been put forth and the errors that have been committed.

What can we say to these things? What can the advocate for apocalyptic study reply to these undeniable facts?

My answer is that the variations and mistakes in the views of interpreters are no argument against the study of the book itself. Because others have missed the road in searching for truth, you and I are not to give up the search altogether and sit down in contented ignorance. Who has not heard of the outrageous and contradictory theories which astronomers, geologists, and physicians have occasionally proposed in their respective sciences? Yet who would think of giving up astronomy, geology, or medicine in despair because of the conflicting tenets and acknowledged mistakes of their professors? Luther and Zwingli differed widely about the Lord's Supper. Cranmer and Hooper differed widely about vestments. Wesley and Toplady differed widely on predestination. Yet no one in his right mind would think of giving up the study of the Christian system because these good men could not agree.

Further, the very mistakes and differences of apocalyptic interpreters are not without their use. They have cleared the field in many directions and shown us what the book of Revelation does *not* mean. In many cases, expositors have shown the weakness of other men's interpretations, even if they have not succeeded in establishing their own. To know what an unfulfilled scriptural prediction does not mean is one step towards knowing what it does mean. When Napoleon, on a dark evening, was overtaken by the rising tide on the sandy shore of the Red Sea, he is said to have ordered his attendants to disperse and ride in different directions, and charged each one to report as he rode whether the water grew shallower or deeper. There was great wisdom in that order. Each man's report was useful. The report of him who found the water deepening was in its way as useful as the report of the finder of the right path. It is much the same with the widely varying expositions of Revelation. It is evident that many of them must be wrong. But all in their way have done good; they have all contributed some spark of light.[44]

---

44 "Among the interpreters of Revelation in the last ages, there is scarce one of note who hath

I would also answer that the differences of apocalyptic interpretations, great as they undoubtedly are, are often magnified and absurdly exaggerated. The common points of agreement among expositors are more in number and greater in importance than commonly supposed. Whether the seals, trumpets, and vials are fulfilled or not, all students of Revelation agree that it predicts judgments on the unconverted and unbelieving. Whether days mean literal days, as some say, or years, as others say, all are agreed that the time of the wicked's success is defined, limited, and fixed by the counsels of God. Whether the beast with horns like a lamb be the papal power or not, nearly all are agreed that Roman Catholic apostasy is foretold in the book and doomed. Whether Christ will come and reign visibly on earth or not, for 1,000 or 365,000 years, all are agreed that He will come again with power and great glory, that the kingdoms of this world will sooner or later become the kingdoms of our God and of His Christ, and that all believers should look and long for their Lord's return. I doubt the opponents of apocalyptic study have given this as much consideration as it deserves.

I freely grant them that the disagreement and inconsistencies of the paths drawn out by the expositors of the book are very many and very great. But I ask them to remember that the great ending point toward which all their lines lead is always one and the same. Oh! If people would remember that mighty ending point and realize the tremendous importance of the end and the breaking up of all things toward which they are racing. Then they would be more anxious to study any book which talks about matters like those contained in Revelation. Then they would be less willing to grab at any excuse to decline apocalyptic study.

The only remaining objection to the study of Revelation which I will note is that which is taken from the mysterious character of a large portion of the book.

It is impossible to deny that Revelation is full of hidden and difficult things. Some of its symbols and emblems the Spirit of God has thought good to interpret and explain. The seven stars, the seven candlesticks, the incense, the fine linen, the waters on which the woman sat, the woman herself – all these and a few more are explained, perhaps as

---

not made some discovery worth knowing." – Sir Isaac Newton in *Observations on Daniel and the Apocalypse of St. John*, 1733.

an illustration of the kind of meaning which should be attached to the symbols of the book generally. But there remains a very large number of visions and emblems which the Spirit has not thought fit to interpret. These symbols are unquestionably dark and mysterious. Even after all the attempts of commentators, both ancient and modern, preterist and futurist, there are still many visions and symbols of Revelation which we do not understand. Elaborate and educated expositions of them have been offered, but they have not been demonstrated and explained satisfactorily enough to demand that we agree with them. If truth be told, we must admit that all the expositions of some parts of Revelation are nothing better than ingenious conjectures. We admire them as we read. We are not prepared to say that they are not true or to furnish a reason for refusing our assent, but they fail to carry conviction with them. We somehow feel the target has not been hit, the lock has not been sprung, the whole truth has not yet been discovered.

But I appeal to common sense and a sense of fairness, and I ask them whether they have a right to expect that such a book as the book of Revelation can in its very nature be anything but dark and mysterious.

Here is a prophetic book that spans the mighty gulf between the end of the first century and the day of judgment, a book which was given to show God's dealings with the church and the world during a space of nearly two thousand years. It is a book that points to the rise and fall of empires and kingdoms with all the attendant wars and tumults over a third part of the habitable globe, and a book that, above all, does not tell its story in simple, plain, matter-of-fact narration, but clothes it in majestic visions, symbols, emblems, figures, and similitudes.

Here we are reading this book during a lifetime of seventy years at most, with all the cares and anxieties of this world pressing upon us, with our understanding corrupted by the fall, and with a heart that is naturally earthly and sensual, and even after conversion is weak and deceitful. We know little of ourselves, know little of contemporary history, and find constantly how hard it is to discover the real truth about events happening in our own day. Is it likely then, is it probable, that we would find the book of Revelation any less mysterious and hard to understand? Can anyone doubt the answer?

The plain truth is that we are like children watching some mighty building in the process of construction. They see a thousand operations which they are utterly unable to comprehend or explain. They see scaffolding and stones, iron and brick, mortar and timber, and rubbish. They hear noise and hammering and cutting and chipping. It seems to their eyes a vast scene of hopeless confusion. And yet to the eye of the architect all is order, system, and progress. He sees the end from the beginning. He knows exactly what is going on.

It is much the same with us trying to pass judgment on the application of many of the apocalyptic visions. We are like those who stand on the outward surface of a sphere. The range of our mental vision is exceedingly limited. We know so little and see so little beyond our own circle. The very pages of history are so often full of inaccuracies and lies that we are really very poor judges of the question as to whether visions have been fulfilled or not. More light, I believe, may be coming before the end. Many of the mysteries may be unfolded and unsealed. But as to any certainty about the meaning of all parts of the Apocalypse, when I see how little certainty there is about anything just one thousand miles from us in distance or one hundred years in time, I admit I do not look for it until the Lord comes.

Let me turn for a moment to those who secretly wonder why the book of Revelation was not written more plainly, and why things of such vast interest to the church have been purposely clothed in the mysterious garb of symbol, allegory, and vision.

I might easily remind such persons of Bishop Sherlock's[45] remark on this very point: "To inquire why the ancient prophecies are not clearer, is like inquiring why God has not given us more reason, or made us as wise as the angels." But I will go further and use an argument that has often proved satisfactory to my own mind and silenced the speculative questionings of a curious spirit.

I ask, Can you not see wisdom and mercy in the darkness which it has pleased God to throw around the prophetic history of His church? You wonder in your own heart why the things to come were not more clearly revealed. But consider for a moment how fearfully deadening and depressing it would have been to the early Christians if they had been able to see clearly the long ages of darkness and corruption which

---

45 Thomas Sherlock (1678–1761) was a bishop in the Church of England.

were to elapse before the Lord returned. Reflect for a moment on how much unhappiness early church believers were spared by not knowing for certain the events which were to take place. If humble saints in the days of imperial persecution could have dreamed of the eighteen weary centuries during which the saints had to wait for their Lord from heaven, they might have sat down in outright despair. If Polycarp had foreseen the present state of Asia Minor, or Ignatius that of Syria, or Chrysostom that of Constantinople, or Irenaeus that of France, or Athanasius that of Egypt, or Augustine that of Africa – their hands might well have trembled and their knees given out.

Count the dark and painful pages of which there are so many in the annals of church history. List all the heresies, false doctrines, and apostasies of which there has been such a vigorous growth – Arianism and Gnosticism and Romanism and their related errors. Think about the centuries of ignorance and superstition before the Reformation, and of coldness and formality since Luther's generation passed away. Count the crimes which have been perpetrated in the name of Christianity – the massacres, the burnings, the persecutions within the church, and do not forget the Waldensians, the Albigenses, the Spanish Inquisition, the slaughter of the Huguenots, and the fires of Smithfield. Do all this faithfully and I think you will come to the conclusion that it was wise mercy which drew so thick a veil over things to come. Wise mercy showed the early Christians a light in the distance but did not tell them how far away it was. Wise mercy pointed out the far-off harbor lights but not the miles of stormy sea between. Wise mercy revealed enough to make them work and hope and wait. But wise mercy did not tell all that was still to be fulfilled before the end.

> Reflect for a moment on how much unhappiness early church believers were spared by not knowing for certain the events which were to take place.

Do we tell our little children in their early years every trial, pain, and misery that they may have to go through before they die? Do we fill their tender ears with the particulars of every bodily disease they may have to endure and every struggle for success in life in which they may have to engage? Do we distress their young souls by describing every bereavement they may have to endure or the ugliness and distortion on every deathbed they may have to watch? We do not do it because they could not understand our meaning and could not bear the thought of it if they did. In the same way, it seems to me, the Lord Jesus deals with His people in the apocalyptic vision. He keeps back the full revelation of all they must go through until the time when He sees they can bear it. He considers our frame. He teaches and reveals as we are able to bear.

The most powerful argument in reply to those who object to the study of Revelation is the simple promise of the Word of God. The predictions of Revelation may seem to many improbable and absurd. The differences and mistakes of interpreters may fill others with disgust and dislike of the very name of apocalyptic study. The acknowledged mysteriousness and confessed difficulties of the book may incline many to shrink from reading it. But there the book stands, part of those Scriptures which are all given by inspiration and all profitable. And there at the beginning of the book stands a promise and an encouragement to the reader and hearer: *Blessed is he that readeth, and they that hear.* These words, no doubt, were spoken in anticipation of the objections that people would raise against the study of the book. Give these words their full weight. Fall back on them when all other arguments fail. They are a reserve which will never yield, never give way. God has said it and will make it good. *Blessed is he that readeth, and they that hear the words of this prophecy.*

Useful lessons that the book of Revelation teaches

This is an important point and I want you to establish it in your mind: the book of Revelation is an eminently profitable book for every reader of the Bible to study. It is a fountain to which the poorest and most unlearned will never go in vain.

There are many blessed and comforting truths scattered up and down all over the book of Revelation which are intelligible to the simplest comprehension, yet also full of food for the most spiritual mind. God has mercifully ordered the composition of the book so that there is hardly a chapter from which you may not draw some striking and edifying thought. You may not be skilled in interpreting visions. You may have no idea of the meaning of seals or trumpets or vials, of the two witnesses, of the woman fleeing into the wilderness, or of the first or second beast. But if you persevere in humble prayer and study of the whole book, you will find in almost every page verses which will richly repay your pains. They will shine out on you like stars in the dark vault of heaven in a moonless night. They will refresh you like an oasis in the wilderness and make it impossible for you to say, "All is barren, there is nothing here." As you walk by the deep waters of the mysterious book, they will sparkle like precious stones on the shore and make you feel that your journey in search of treasure is not in vain.[46]

Let me select a few examples to show what I mean.

There is much about *the Lord Jesus Christ* in Revelation. There are names and titles and expressions about Him there that we find nowhere else. There is new light thrown on His offices, His power, and His care for His people. Surely this alone is no small matter. To know Jesus is life eternal. To abide in Jesus is to be fruitful. If we are indeed born of the Spirit, we can never hear too much about our Savior, our Good Shepherd, our High Priest, and our Great Physician. If our hearts are right in the sight of God, we can never hear too much about our King. Like snow in summer and good news from a far country, so are any fresh tidings about Christ.

There is much about the desperate *corruption of human nature* in Revelation. There is evidence on this subject in the epistles to the seven churches and the repeated accounts of the incorrigibleness and unrepentance of the nations of the earth under judgment, which we will all do well to take to heart. We need to know well our own sinfulness and weakness. The spring of all humility, thankfulness, grateful love for Christ, and a close walk with God is a real, thorough, scriptural knowledge of the wickedness of our own hearts. None will ever build high who does not begin low. The soul that loves much is the soul that feels its debt is great and that much has been forgiven.

There is much about *hell* in Revelation. There are many terrifying expressions which show its reality, its misery, its eternity, its certainty. How important it is to have clear views on this serious subject today!

---

46 "It is true, many things in the book of Revelation are obscure, and it is likely that the full clearing of them is not to be expected till God in some singular way shall open them up. Yet there are many clear, edifying, and comfortable passages of God's mind in it, the Holy Ghost mixing them in to be fed upon, to sweeten those passages that are more obscure, and to encourage the reader to search for the meaning of them." – James Durham in *Commentary upon the Book of the Revelation*, 1658.

There is a tendency in some quarters to shrink from asserting the eternity of punishment. That miserable heresy – universalism – seems to be flooding in upon us. Amiable and well-meaning enthusiasts are speaking smooth things about the love of God being lower than hell and the mercy of God excluding the exercise of all His other attributes of justice and holiness. Tenderhearted women and intellectual men are grabbing at the theory that, after all, there is hope in the far distance for everybody, and that Satan's old assertion deserves credit: *Ye shall not surely die.* Oh, beware of this delusion! Do not think you are wiser than the Scriptures. Believe me, it is a profound thing to believe in the reality of hell. Study the apocalyptic visions well and you will find it hard to disbelieve it.

There is much about *heaven* in Revelation. I speak of heaven in the common acceptance of the word: the future home of the saints and people of God. And I say that no book in God's Word tells us so much about heaven as the Apocalypse. And just this should be enough to make us most thankful. What believer in the Lord Jesus does not frequently think on the world to come and the resurrection state? Who that has lost a dear believing friend or relative does not meditate on the life of glory and the place of meeting? Who among the people of God does not frequently imagine that unknown and unvisited home, and strive to picture in his mind's eye what it is like there and how will we spend our time? It is mysterious, no doubt. But nowhere is the veil lifted so much as it is in the book of Revelation.

There is much about *the prospects of the church of Christ* in Revelation. When I speak of the church, I mean the church of the elect, the living body of Christ, whose members are all holy. The pages of the Apocalypse show plainly that the triumphs, the rest, the ease, and the peace of that church are not in this world. Its members must prepare themselves for battles and fighting, trials and persecutions, crosses and afflictions. They must be content to be a little flock, a poor and despised people, until the advent of Christ. Their good things have not yet come. It would be good if believers would learn from Revelation to moderate their expectations from missions, schools, and all other ecclesiastical machinery. Then we would not hear so often of disappointment and despondency and depression among true Christians, especially among ministers. We live in the time when God is taking out a people for Himself. These are the days of election, but not of universal conversion. We are still in the wilderness. The Bridegroom is not yet with us. The days of absence and mourning and separation are not yet past and gone.

There is much in Revelation to show *the folly of depending entirely on the powers of this world* for the advancement of true religion. Many parts of the book show that believers should not look to kings, princes, rich men, or great men for the bringing in and support of the kingdom of Christ. The times are not yet come when kings will literally be the *nursing fathers* (Isaiah 49:23) of the churches. It is striking to observe how often the Apocalypse speaks of them as the enemies of God's cause, not the friends. We need this lesson here in England. With a settled conviction that the principle of an established church is scriptural and sound, I still feel we need reminding that alliance with the powers that be has its disadvantages as well as its advantages to the visible church of Christ. It is apt to engender laziness, apathy, and formality among professing Christians. I firmly believe that the Church of England would have exerted itself more and done more for the world if its members had been more familiar with the book of Revelation and learned from it to expect little from the State.

> There is much in Revelation to show the painful childishness of the vast majority of true Christians all over the world.

There is much in Revelation to show the painful *childishness of the vast majority of true Christians* all over the world. Here we are, the greater part of us, scrambling and wrangling about the merest trifles – contending about forms and ceremonies and outward matters of man's invention as if they were the essentials of Christianity, and talking of order and precedent and custom and routine, while millions of heathen are perishing for lack of knowledge, and myriads of our countrymen are dying as ignorant as the heathen around our own doors. And all this time the eternal purposes of God are rolling on to fulfillment, the kingdoms of this world are on the brink of dissolution, the day of judgment is at hand, and an hour draws near when Episcopacy, Presbyterianism, Congregationalism, state churches, and non-state churches will be swept clean out of the way, and nothing but grace, faith, and heart-holiness will abide and stand the fire. Never do I read the Apocalypse without feeling the excessive littleness of Christians. We are like children busy with our little houses of sand at low water by the seaside. The tide is rising and our houses will soon be gone. We will be fortunate if we escape with our lives!

And last, there is much in Revelation to show *the safety of all true believers in Christ,* whatever may come upon the world. As awful as the woes are of which the Apocalypse speaks, there is not a syllable to show that a hair will fall from the head of any one of God's children. Hidden like Noah in the ark, plucked like Lot from the fiery judgment, withdrawn like Elijah from the reach of their enemies, rescued like Rahab from the ruin all around – believers, at least, may read Revelation without being afraid. The book that looks dark and threatening to the world speaks no terrors to them. Like the wondrous pillar of cloud at Pihahiroth (Exodus 14:2), it may fill the mind of an ungodly man with gloom, but like the same cloud, it will give light by night to the people of God.

I have mentioned eight things that are stated plainly and unmistakably in the book of Revelation. There is no mystery about them. They require no deep learning to understand. A humble mind and a prayerful heart are all that are needed to discover them.

The offices of the Lord Jesus Christ Himself, the corruption of man, the reality of hell, the nature of heaven, the prospects of the church, the folly of trusting in princes, the childishness of God's people, the safety of believers in the day of wrath – these are the kinds of subjects we need to be familiar with and know very well. These are the plain lessons that Revelation, even with all its many difficulties, will unfold. If these things are written deeply on our minds, our reading of the Apocalypse will be blessed indeed!

These are also the kinds of things that Satan works hard to keep us from. That old Enemy tries to fill our minds with prejudice against apocalyptic study. He will suggest the evil thought, "It is all mysterious, it is all too deep, we need not read it." Let us resist him in this matter. Let us cling to Revelation more closely every year. Let us never doubt that it is a profitable study for our souls.

I will conclude now with three practical remarks. First, let us thank God that the things needful to salvation are all clear, plain, and devoid of mystery to those with a humble mind. Whatever difficulties there may be in the visions of the Apocalypse, even the most unlearned reader of the Bible will never miss the way to heaven if he seeks to find it in a childlike and prayerful spirit.

The guilt, corruption, and weakness of man is not a hidden thing, like a seal, a trumpet, or a vial. Christ's power and willingness to save and justification by faith in Him are not a dark thing like the number 666. The absolute necessity of a new birth and a thorough change of heart is not an uncertainty like the meaning of the two witnesses. The impossibility of salvation without fitness for heaven is not a mystery like the interpretation of the vision of the four living creatures.

But remember while you thank God for this clear teaching in the things essential to salvation that this very clearness increases your personal responsibility. Even though there is an open door set in front of you, you need to be careful to enter it and be saved.

Listen everyone and understand. I give you a plain warning this day. Do not forget it. You may reach heaven without knowing much about the deep things of the Apocalypse, but you will never get there without the saving knowledge of Christ and a new heart. You must be born again. You must renounce your own righteousness and acknowledge yourself a sinner. You must wash in the fountain of Christ's blood. You must be clothed in the garment of Christ's righteousness. You must take up the cross of Christ and follow Him.

> You must wash in the fountain of Christ's blood. You must be clothed in the garment of Christ's righteousness. You must take up the cross of Christ and follow Him.

These are the things absolutely necessary. These are the things without which no man, learned or unlearned, high or low, can ever be saved.

Do not rest until you know these things by experience. Without them you may know the whole list of apocalyptic commentaries and be familiar with all that Mede, Brightman, Cressener, Daubuz, Durham, Cuninghame, Woodhouse, Elliot, Alford, and Garratt have written on the subject, and yet rise at the last day a lost soul – knowing much intellectually, like the devils, but, like the devils, be ruined forever.

Let me also tell all students of the book of Revelation to beware of dogmatism and overconfidence when expressing and maintaining your views of the meaning of its more mysterious portions.

Nothing has brought more discredit on the study of prophecy than the excessive rashness and overbearing confidence with which many of its advocates have promoted their own interpretations and impugned the expositions of others. Too many have written and talked as if they had a special revelation from heaven and as if it were impossible for anyone else to have any common sense if they did not see it in the same way.[47]

Let us all watch our hearts and be on our guard against this spirit. Dogmatism is a great trap that Satan lays in our way when he cannot prevent us from studying the Apocalypse. Let us not fall into it. Instead, let us pray for a spirit of modesty and humility when offering our interpretations of symbolic prophecy. Let us allow that we may possibly be wrong and that others may possibly be right. Believe me, we all need this caution. We are prone to be most positive when we have least warrant for our assertions simply because our pride whispers that our credibility is at stake, and since we made our statements mainly on the authority of our own judgment, we are specially bound to defend them.

Happy is that student of prophecy who is willing to confess that there are many things about which he is still ignorant. Happier still, but more uncommon, is the one who is able to use those three hardest words in the English language: "I was mistaken."

Finally, let all believers take comfort in the thought that the end to which all things are coming is clear, plain, and unmistakable. There may still be judgments in store for the world that we know nothing about. There may be *distress of nations, with perplexity* (Luke 21:25) far exceeding anything we have yet heard of, read, or seen. There may be more grievous wars and famines and pestilences and persecution still to come.

But the end is sure. In a little while He that will come, will come and will not tarry. The kings of the earth may struggle and contend for their

---

[47] "Joseph Mede, the most learned and able interpreter of prophecy that this country can name among its divines, was remarkable for his modesty and humility. In a letter of his to Dr. Twiss, speaking of the leisurely and deliberate progress he made in his exposition of Apocalypse, he adds these words, 'I am by nature dilatory in all things, but in this let no man blame me if I take more pause than ordinary; for it has sunk deeply into my mind, that rashly to be the author of a false interpretation of Scripture is to take God's name in vain in a high degree.'" – Joseph Mede in *Mede's Works*, 1672.

own worldly interests, but sooner or later the kingdoms of this world will become the kingdoms of our God and of His Christ. There will be an eternal peace. He will come and take possession, *whose right it is* (Ezekiel 21:27). The dominion and power will be given to the saints of the Most High, and of the increase of their peace there will be no end.

Oh, remember this! To gain our souls we must endure. In every trying time do as Luther did – repeat the forty-sixth psalm:

> *God is our refuge and strength, a very present help in trouble. Therefore will not we fear, though the earth be removed, and though the mountains be carried into the midst of the sea; though the waters thereof roar and be troubled, though the mountains shake with the swelling thereof. Selah. There is a river, the streams whereof shall make glad the city of God, the holy place of the tabernacles of the most High. God is in the midst of her; she shall not be moved: God shall help her, and that right early. The heathen raged, the kingdoms were moved: he uttered his voice, the earth melted. The* LORD *of hosts is with us; the God of Jacob is our refuge. Selah. Come, behold the works of the* LORD, *what desolations he hath made in the earth. He maketh wars to cease unto the end of the earth; he breaketh the bow, and cutteth the spear in sunder; he burneth the chariot in the fire. Be still, and know that I am God: I will be exalted among the heathen, I will be exalted in the earth. The* LORD *of hosts is with us; the God of Jacob is our refuge. Selah.*

Chapter 7

And So All Israel Shall Be Saved

And so all Israel shall be saved: as it is written, There shall come out of Sion the Deliverer, and shall turn away ungodliness from Jacob. (Romans 11:26)

This is one of the great unfulfilled prophecies of Scripture. More than eighteen centuries have rolled around since Paul wrote these words. During that period, many marvelous and unexpected events have taken place. The world has often been convulsed and turned upside down. Empires and kingdoms have risen and fallen. Nations and peoples have decayed and passed away. Visible churches have disappeared and no longer have influence in the world. But as of yet, Paul's prediction is still not accomplished. *All Israel shall be saved* remains yet unfulfilled.

To a plain man, not hampered by the interpretation of tradition, the words of this prophecy appear very simple. It is not like the temple which Ezekiel saw in a vision: a dark and obscure thing, of which we may say as Daniel said of another vision, *I heard, but I understood not* (Daniel 12:8). It is not presented to us under the veil of emblems, like the seals, trumpets, vials, and beasts in Revelation, about which men will probably never be of one mind until the Lord comes, and the wisest commentator can only conjecture. It is nothing like this! The sentence before us is a simple, direct proposition, and I firmly believe it means exactly what it appears to mean. Let us analyze it.

And so. That means, as Parkhurst says, "and then, then at length." It is an expression of time rather than manner. It is like Acts 7:8: *And so Abraham begat Isaac,* and 1 Thessalonians 4:17: *And so shall we ever be with the Lord.*

Israel shall be saved. That means the Jewish nation and people. It cannot possibly mean the gentiles, because they are mentioned in the verse which directly precedes our text in distinct contrast to the Jews: *Blindness in part is happened to Israel, until the fulness of the Gentiles be come in* (Romans 11:25).

All Israel. This means the whole people or nation of the Jews. It cannot possibly mean a small elect remnant. In this very chapter Israel and *the election* out of Israel are mentioned in contrast to one another: *Israel hath not obtained that which he seeketh for; but the election hath obtained it, and the rest were blinded* (Romans 11:7).

Shall be saved. That means they will be redeemed from their present unbelief and have their eyes opened to see and believe the true Messiah. They will be delivered from their low estate and restored to the favor of God, and will become a holy nation and a blessing to the world.

The interpretation complete, I will now remark on four points regarding Israel that all friends of the Jews should keep fresh in their minds. Trite and familiar as they may seem to some, they are overlooked and forgotten by others. But I do not hesitate to say that a firm grasp of these four points is the foundation of any real and abiding interest in the Jewish subject and cause.

First, consider the very peculiar past history of this Israel, which is one day to be saved. For the facts of that history, I will simply refer you to the Bible. Whatever modern skepticism may say, the story of Israel that the venerable old Book records is as trustworthy as the story of any ancient nation in the world. We have no more basis for disputing its accuracy than for disputing the accounts of Egypt, Assyria, Persia, or Greece related by Herodotus. On the contrary, there is continually accumulating evidence that the Old Testament memoirs of the Jewish people are thoroughly trustworthy and true.

Israel, we find, was for nearly fifteen hundred years more favored and privileged by God than any nation in the world. David might well say, *What one nation in the earth is like thy people, even like Israel, whom God went to redeem for a people to himself?* (2 Samuel 7:23). It was the only nation on earth to which God was pleased to reveal Himself: *Unto them were committed the oracles of God* (Romans 3:2). While all other nations were permitted to walk in their own ways and to live in moral and spiritual darkness, the Jews alone enjoyed an immense amount of light and knowledge. The humblest priest in Solomon's temple was a far better theologian than Homer. Daniel, Ezra, and Nehemiah knew more about God than Socrates, Plato, Pythagoras, and Cicero all put together. The Jews were brought out of Egypt by miraculous intervention, planted in Palestine, one of the choicest corners of the earth, and fenced off and separated from other nations by peculiar customs and ceremonies. They were supplied with a moral law from heaven so perfect, that even to this day nothing can be added to it or taken from it. They were taught to worship God with ceremonial rites and ordinances, which, however burdensome they may seem to us, were admirably adapted to human nature at that early stage of man's history, and calculated to train them for a higher dispensation. They were constantly warned and instructed by prophets and protected and defended by miracles. In short, if mercies and kindnesses alone could make people good, no nation on earth should have been so good as Israel. While Egypt and Babylon and Greece worshipped the works of their own hands, Jews alone were worshippers of the one true God.

But Israel, we find, was a people always prone to backsliding and falling away from God. Again and again, they fell into idolatry and wickedness and abandoned the Lord God of their fathers. Again and again, they were punished for their sins and delivered into the hands of the nations around them. Midianites, Philistines, Ammonites, Syrians, Assyrians, and Babylonians were rods by which they were repeatedly scourged. From the time of the Judges down to the end of Chronicles, we see a sorrowful record of constantly recurring rebellions against God and constantly recurring punishments. Never, apparently, was there a nation so stubborn and obstinate, so ready to forget instruction, so mercifully dealt with, and yet so unrepentant and unbelieving.

Finally, we find Israel at the end of fifteen hundred years given up by God to a fearful punishment and allowed to reap the consequences of their own sins. After repeatedly rejecting God's prophets, they brought their wickedness to a head by rejecting God's only begotten Son. They refused their true King, the Son of David, and would have no king but Caesar. Then at last the cup of their iniquity was full and Jerusalem was given up to the Romans. The holy and beautiful temple was burned. The Mosaic services were brought to an end. The Jews themselves were deprived of their land and scattered all over the earth.

The whole history is wonderful, peculiar, and unlike anything else that is recorded and known by man. Never was a people so peculiarly favored and so peculiarly punished. Never did any nation at one time rise so high and at another fall so low. Never was there such a tremendous proof given to the world of the depravity of human nature and the incessant tendency of man to moral and spiritual decay. Those who are fond of telling us in modern times that kindness and love are sufficient to regenerate man and keep man good are always forgetting the mighty lesson that is taught us by the history of the Jews. The corruption of man is a far worse disease than your modern philosophers suppose. Israel was surrounded by mercies and loving-kindnesses, yet Israel fell. Never forget that.

Consider also the very peculiar position which Israel as a nation occupies at the present day. In handling this point I will first simply refer to facts that are open to the observation of every intelligent and well-informed person on earth, whether a believer or not. I will close my Bible for a moment, and I will not ask you to listen to texts. I will only offer facts and challenge you to deny them if you can.

I assert, then, that the Jews are at this moment a peculiar people and utterly separate from all other people on the face of the earth. They fulfill the prophecy of Hosea: *The children of Israel shall abide many days without a king, and without a prince, and without a sacrifice* (Hosea 3:4). For eighteen hundred years they have been scattered over the globe, without a country, without a government, and without a capital city. They are strangers and aliens everywhere, often fiercely persecuted, and vilely treated. Yet to this moment they continue as a distinct, isolated, and separate nation, far more so than any nation on the earth. The wonderful words of that strange prophet Balaam, which God obliged him to speak, are still literally true: *The people shall dwell alone, and shall not be reckoned among the nations* (Numbers 23:9).

Of what other nation or people on earth can that be said? I answer, confidently, none. When Nineveh and Babylon and Tyre and the hundred-gated Thebes of Egypt and Susa and Persepolis and Carthage and Palmyra were destroyed, what became of their inhabitants and subjects? We can give no answer. No doubt they were carried away captive and dispersed. But where are they now? No one can tell. When Saxons, Danes, Normans, and Flemings under the persecution of Alva, and Frenchmen after the edict of Nantes settled down in our own England, what became of them? They were all gradually absorbed into our own population and have generally lost all their national distinctions, except, perhaps, in some cases, their names. But nothing of the sort has ever happened to the Jews; they are still entirely distinct and never absorbed.

Even in matters of relatively minor importance, there is to this very day an extraordinary separateness between the Jews and any other family of mankind on the face of the globe. Time seems unable to erase the difference. At the end of eighteen centuries, they are a separate people. Physically, they are separate. Who does not know the Jewish type of features? Even a man like Mr. Lawrence, in his work on physiology, is obliged to admit that "the Jews exhibit one of the most striking instances of national formation unaltered by the most remarkable changes."[48] In customs and habits they are separate. The tenacity with which they cling to their Saturday Sabbath and the feasts of their law might put Christians to shame. Even in their political influence they are strangely separate. The extraordinary financial power which they exercise in all the money markets of the world enables them to sway the actions of governments to an extent that few can imagine. In short, if there ever was a people distinct, marked, cut off, and separate from others, that people is Israel. Though they have lived among the gentiles for eighteen centuries, they are still as distinct from the gentiles as black is distinct from white, and seem to be as incapable of mixture or absorption as oil is incapable of being absorbed into or mixed with water.

---

48 William Lawrence, *Lectures on Physiology, Zoology, and the Natural History of Man*, 3rd edition, 1819, p. 468.

How do we account for this? How do we explain the unique and peculiar position that the Jewish people occupy in the world? Why is it that unlike the Saxons, Danes, Normans, Flemings, and French, this singular race, though broken to pieces like a wreck, still floats alone on the waters of the globe amidst its 1.5 billion inhabitants? How is it that after a lapse of eighteen hundred years it is not destroyed, crushed, evaporated, amalgamated, nor lost sight of, but lives to this day as separate and distinct as it was when the Arch of Titus was built at Rome?

I have not the least idea how questions like these are answered by those who deny the divine authority of Scripture. In all my reading I never met with an honest attempt to answer them from the unhappy camp of unbelievers. In fact, it is my firm conviction that among the many difficulties of unbelief there is hardly one more insurmountable than the separate continuance of the Jewish nation. It is a burdensome stone which your modern skeptical writers may pretend to despise but cannot lift or remove out of their way. You would find that God has many witnesses to the truth of the Bible if you would only examine them and listen to their evidence. But there is no witness so irrefutable as one whom He always keeps standing up, and living, and moving before the eyes of mankind. That witness is the Jew.

The question, however, about the exceptional and peculiar position of the Jewish people is one that never need puzzle anyone who believes the Bible. Once you open that Book and study its contents, the knot which so completely baffles the skeptic is one that you can easily untie. The inspired volume which you have in your hands supplies a full and complete explanation. Search it with an honest determination to put a literal meaning on its prophetic portions and to reject traditional interpretation, and the difficulty will vanish.

I contend that the peculiar position which Israel occupies in the earth is easily explicable in the light of Holy Scripture. They are a people reserved and kept separate by God for a grand and special purpose. That purpose is to make them in the latter days a means of exhibiting to the world God's hatred of sin and unbelief and God's almighty power and compassion. They are kept separate so that they may finally be saved, converted, and restored to their own land. They are reserved and preserved in order that God may show in them, to angels and men, how greatly He hates sin and yet how greatly He can forgive and convert. Never will that be actualized as it will be in that day when *all Israel shall be saved.*

Consider the very peculiar future prospects of Israel. The most distinctive condition of the Jews at the present time, we have seen, is most painful and instructive; they are still lying under the just displeasure of God. Because they despised His prophets and rejected His messages, because they would not believe the voice of His Scriptures read to them every Sabbath day, because they killed the Prince of life and were His betrayers and murderers – for all these reasons His enormous wrath is come on them, and for a time they are cast off and rejected. Like Cain, they killed their holy Brother, and like Cain, they are fugitives and vagabonds on earth and bear the mark of God's displeasure. They murdered the Messiah and His blood is upon them and their children. And their eyes are still blinded. The veil is still over their hearts. They stand before the world at this moment like a light at the top of a hill, a perpetual witness that nothing is so offensive to God as unbelief, formalism, self-righteousness, and abuse of privileges. This is their present position. But what are their future prospects? What can they look forward to? Let us turn once more to the Bible to see.

> The history of Israel has not yet come to an end.

The history of Israel has not yet come to an end. There is another wonderful chapter still to be unfolded to mankind. The Scripture tells us expressly that a time is coming when the position of Israel will be entirely changed, and they will once more be restored to the favor of God. No Scripture in that Book will ever be broken, no prediction will ever fail. In this Book, I read that when the heart of Israel *shall turn to the Lord, the vail shall be taken away* (2 Corinthians 3:16). I read that a day is coming when God says, *I will pour upon the house of David, and upon the inhabitants of Jerusalem, the spirit of grace and of supplications: and they shall look upon me whom they have pierced, and they shall mourn for him, as one mourneth for his only son* (Zechariah 12:10). I read that *in that day there shall be a fountain opened to the house of David and to the inhabitants of Jerusalem for sin and for uncleanness* (Zechariah 13:1). I beg you to remember that the primary application of these prophecies of Zechariah belongs literally to the Jews. I read, also, that God says to Israel in Ezekiel,

> *For I will take you from among the heathen, and gather you out of all countries, and will bring you into your own land. Then will I sprinkle clean water upon you, and ye shall be clean: from all your filthiness, and from all your idols, will I cleanse you. A new heart also will I give you, and a new spirit will I put within you: and I will take away the stony heart out of your flesh, and I will give you an heart of flesh. And I will put my spirit within you, and cause you to walk in my statutes, and ye shall keep my judgments, and do them. And ye shall dwell in the land that I gave to your fathers; and ye shall be my people, and I will be your God. I will also save you from all your uncleannesses: and I will call for the corn, and will increase it, and lay no famine upon you. And I will multiply the fruit of the tree, and the increase of the field, that ye shall receive no more reproach of famine among the heathen. Then shall ye remember your own evil ways, and your doings that were not good, and shall lothe yourselves in your own sight for your iniquities and for your abominations. Not for your sakes do I this, saith the Lord God, be it known unto you: be ashamed and confounded for your own ways, O house of Israel. Thus saith the Lord God; In the day that I shall have cleansed you from all your iniquities I will also cause you to dwell in the cities, and the wastes shall be builded. And the desolate land shall be tilled, whereas it lay desolate in the sight of all that passed by. And they shall say, This land that was desolate is become like the garden of Eden; and the waste and desolate and ruined cities are become fenced, and are inhabited. Then the heathen that are left round about you shall know that I the Lord build the ruined places, and plant that that was desolate: I the Lord have spoken it, and I will do it. Thus saith the Lord God; I will yet for this be enquired of by the house of Israel, to do it for them; I will increase them with men like a flock.*

As the holy flock, as the flock of Jerusalem in her solemn feasts; so shall the waste cities be filled with flocks of men: and they shall know that I am the LORD. (Ezekiel 36:24-38)

Once more I remind you that this wonderful passage *primarily* belongs to the Jews. No doubt the church of Christ may secondarily make a spiritual use of it. But let us never forget that the Holy Spirit first caused it to be written concerning Israel.

I would run out of time if I attempted to quote all the passages of Scripture in which the future history of Israel is revealed. Isaiah, Jeremiah, Ezekiel, Hosea, Joel, Amos, Obadiah, Micah, Zephaniah, Zechariah – all declare the same thing. All predict, with more or less detail, that in the end of this dispensation the Jews will be restored to their own land and to the favor of God. I do not say my interpretation of Scripture in this matter is infallible. I am well aware that many excellent Christians do not see the subject as I do. I can only say that, to my eyes, the future salvation of Israel as a people, their return to Palestine, and their national conversion to God appear as clearly and plainly revealed as any prophecy in God's Word.

> Let it be enough to believe that whatever God has said concerning Israel, God will do in His own good time.

I will not offer an opinion concerning the time when Israel will finally be saved. No doubt there are many signs of the times which deserve the serious attention of all Christians, and it would be easy to list them. But we are always bad judges of anything that happens under our own eyes. We are apt to attach an exaggerated importance to it for the simple reason that we ourselves are affected by it. Let it be enough to believe that whatever God has said concerning Israel, God will do in His own good time. Do not be in a hurry to fix dates. Those last words of our Master are very instructive; when the disciple said, *Wilt thou at this time restore again the kingdom to Israel?* He answered, *It is not for you to know the times or the seasons, which the Father hath put in his own power* (Acts 1:6-7). To study prophecy is useful and brings a special blessing, but to become prophets ourselves is not wise and brings discredit on the cause of Christianity.

We should not pry too closely into the manner in which the complete salvation of Israel will be accomplished. We must avoid rash speculation and conjecture. My opinion is that Scripture seems to point out that Israel will not be restored and converted without an immense amount of affliction – affliction far exceeding that which preceded their deliverance from Egypt. I see a great deal in the words of Daniel: *There shall be a time of trouble, such as never was since there was a nation even to that same time: and at that time thy people shall be delivered, every one that shall be found written in the book* (Daniel 12:1). I believe the words of Zechariah are yet to be fulfilled: *It shall come to pass, that in all the land, saith the* Lord, *two parts therein shall be cut off and die; but the third shall be left therein. And I will bring the third part through the fire, and will refine them as silver is refined, and will try them as gold is tried: they shall call on my name, and I will hear them: I will say, It is my people: and they shall say, The* Lord *is my God* (Zechariah 13:8-9). But I freely confess that these are deep things. Without diving into too many details, it is enough for you and me to know that Israel will be restored to their own land and will be converted and saved.

Let me close this branch of my subject with the apostle Paul's words: *O the depth of the riches both of the wisdom and knowledge of God! how unsearchable are his judgments, and his ways past finding out!* (Romans 11:33), and let us grasp firmly the great principle recorded by Jeremiah:

> *Fear not thou, O my servant Jacob, and be not dismayed,*
> *O Israel: for, behold, I will save thee from afar off, and thy*
> *seed from the land of their captivity; and Jacob shall return,*
> *and be in rest and at ease, and none shall make him afraid.*
> *Fear thou not, O Jacob my servant, saith the* Lord: *for I am*
> *with thee; for I will make a full end of all the nations whither*
> *I have driven thee: but I will not make a full end of thee,*
> *but correct thee in measure; yet will I not leave thee wholly*
> *unpunished.* (Jeremiah 46:27-28)

Lastly, I ask you to consider the peculiar debt which Christians owe to Israel. I will touch on this subject briefly because it is one with which most people are familiar. But it is one about which we all need to be reminded and is of such importance that I dare not pass over it altogether.

That every Christian is a debtor and under solemn obligation to do good to his fellow man is one of the great first principles of the gospel. Those who just go to church but never read their Bibles, or truly pray, or think seriously about their souls may not understand this. They are apt to say with Cain, "*Am I my brother's keeper?* Let everyone mind his own business." But those who are taught by the Holy Spirit, who feel their sins, who know their obligation to Christ, and have tasted the comfort of peace with God will long to do good to others. They will feel for those who are living without God and without Christ. They will say, "I am a debtor to Greek and Barbarian, to Africa and India and China. What can I do to save souls and make others share my blessings?"

Now I ask you to seriously consider whether or not you are under special obligation to the Jew. There are three peculiar reasons why we should give more than ordinary care to Israel.

1. To whom do we owe our Bible? Who wrote that Book which is a lamp to so many feet and a lantern to so many paths and that provides comfort both in life and in death? I answer that every book in the Old and New Testaments, unless we exclude Job, was written by Jews. The pens that wrote the inspired words of the Holy Spirit were held by Jewish fingers. The hands used to forge this matchless sword of the Spirit were Jewish hands. Every time we read that wondrous volume whose nature and existence no unbeliever can explain away, and every time we draw out of it doctrine, correction, reproof, and instruction in righteousness, our eyes fall on matter which passed through Jewish minds. The texts which we live by now, the texts, when sight and hearing fail us, that we will cling to by memory in death and will be the staff in our hand when we go down into the cold river – these texts were first put down in black and white by Jews. Is this nothing?

2. To whom do we owe the first preaching of the gospel? Who were the first to go into the world and proclaim to

the gentiles the unsearchable riches of Christ? Again, I answer, they were all Jews. The men who first turned the world upside down, who deprived heathen temples of their worshippers and put to silence the philosophers of Greece and Rome, who made kings and rulers tremble on their judgment seats and made the name of the crucified Jesus of Nazareth more influential than the name of Caesar – they were all children of Israel. They soon passed away. Many of them died for their preaching, and the lamp they lit was taken up by multitudes of converted gentiles who walked in their steps. But the fact remains, that the first to begin that blessed work on which the very life of a church depends even now, the preaching of the gospel, were all Jews. Where would Europe be at this moment if it had not been for an invasion of Jewish preachers who obeyed the call to come over and help? Surely this also is something.

3. Above all, what will we say about the fact that the Savior, when He condescended to come into the world, was born to a Jewish woman? When that grand mystery that so many shrug off and hold back – the incarnation – took place, when the Word was made flesh and dwelt among us, the virgin who miraculously conceived and bore a son was a virgin of the house of David. No royal family of Assyria or Persia or Greece or Rome was chosen for this honor. That precious blood shed on Calvary for our redemption was the blood which flowed from the body of one who was a man in all things like ourselves, except for sin, and took a man's nature by being born of an Israelite woman. The seed of the woman that bruised the serpent's head, the Mediator between God and man, the Almighty Friend of sinners – when He *took upon him the form of a servant* (Philippians 2:7), though equal to God, was pleased to take the form of a Jew. *He took on him the seed of Abraham* (Hebrews 2:16).

These facts, I am sure, make up a peculiar claim on Christians. In the light of the Bible, the preaching of the gospel, and the person of Christ,

I boldly say that Christians owe a peculiar debt to Israel. If there is such a thing as gratitude in the world, every gentile church on earth is under heavy obligation to the Jews.

But how can our debt be paid? That question can be answered in two ways.

On the one hand, we may pay our debt directly by using every reasonable effort to bring the gospel to the Jews in every part of the globe. No doubt they need to be approached with peculiar wisdom, delicacy, and care. They are not to be treated as heathen but as men who already hold half the truth, and who believe the Old Testament like ourselves, although they do not see and accept its full meaning. But experience proves that those who endeavor to lead Israel to the true Messiah, the Christ of God, with love and patience, will be encouraged.

Now, as in the apostles' times, though the nation as a whole remains unbelieving, *there is a remnant according to the election of grace* (Romans 11:5). There is abundant encouragement to do what the London Society for Promoting Christianity amongst the Jews does and preach the gospel directly to the Jews. If Saul the Pharisee was converted and made a Christian, I do not know why we should despair of the conversion of any Israelite upon earth – in Europe, Asia, Africa, or America.

On the other hand, we may all pay our debt indirectly by striving to remove stumbling blocks which now lie between the Jews and Christianity. I believe that nothing perhaps so hardens Israel in unbelief as the sins and inconsistencies of professing Christians. The name of Christ is too often blasphemed among Jews because of the conduct of many who call themselves Christians. We repel Israel from the door of life and disgust them by our behavior. Idolatry among Roman Catholics, skepticism among Protestants, neglect of the Old Testament, contempt for the doctrine of the atonement, shameless Sabbath-breaking, widespread immorality, all these things, we may be sure, have a deep effect on the Jews. They have eyes and they can see. The name of Christ is discredited and dishonored among them by the practice of those who have been baptized in Christ's name. The more boldly and decidedly all true Christians set their faces against the things I have just named, and wash their hands of any complicity with them, the more likely they are to find their efforts to promote Christianity among the Jews prosperous and successful.

And now let me conclude with a few plain words of application. I ask all of you to take an interest in and participate in the cause of the Jews' Society and the Jewish concern for the following reasons.

Concern yourself with Israel because of the **important position it occupies in Scripture.** Cultivate the habit of reading prophecy with an eye to the literal meaning of its proper names. Cast aside the old traditional idea that Jacob, Israel, Judah, Jerusalem, and Zion must always mean the gentile church, and that predictions about the second advent are to be taken spiritually and the first-advent predictions literally. Be just and honest and fair. If you expect the Jews to take the fifty-third chapter of Isaiah literally, be sure you take the fifty-fourth, the sixtieth, and the sixty-second literally also. The Protestant reformers were not perfect. I say on no point were they so wrong as in the interpretation of Old Testament prophecy. Even our venerable authorized version of the Bible has many tables of contents in the prophetic books, which are, sadly, calculated to mislead. When the revised version comes out, I hope we will see a great improvement in this respect.

You should take an interest in the Jewish subject because of **the times in which we live.** You would have to be blind to not see how much attention politicians and statesmen are concentrating on the countries around Palestine. The strange position of things in Egypt, the formation of the Suez Canal, the occupation of Cyprus, the project of the Euphrates railway, the drying up of the Turkish empire, the trigonometrical survey of Palestine – what curious phenomena these are! What do they mean? What is going to happen next? He that believes will not make haste. I will not pretend to decide. But I think I hear the voice of God saying, "Remember the Jews, look to Jerusalem."

Then, participate in the cause of caring for the Jews because of **the special blessing which seems to be given to those who care for Israel.** Few ministers of Christ have been so useful of late and made a greater mark on the world than the ring of well-known men that includes Charles Simeon, Edward Bickersteth, Haldane Stewart, Dr. Marsh, Robert M'Cheyne, and Hugh M'Neile. They were men of very different gifts and minds, but they had one common feature in their religion: they loved the cause of the Jews. In them was the promise fulfilled: *They shall prosper that love thee* (Psalm 122:6).

Take an interest in the Jewish subject because of **its close connection with the second advent of Christ and the close of this dispensation.** Is it not written, *When the* L<small>ORD</small> *shall build up Zion, he shall appear in his glory* (Psalm 102:16)? *If the casting away of [Israel] be the reconciling of the world, what shall the receiving of them be, but life from the dead?* (Romans 11:15). The words which the angel Gabriel addressed to the Virgin Mary have not yet been fulfilled: *He shall reign over the house of Jacob for ever; and of his kingdom there shall be no end* (Luke 1:33).

Last, let us annually **support that great institution, the Jews' Society,** with our money and our prayers. Our money will be used well by an old and faithful servant of Christ who does Christ's work in Christ's own way. Our prayers are applied well if given for a cause which is so near our Master's heart. The time is short. The night of the world is drawing near. If ever there is "a nation born in a day," that nation will be Israel. Let us pray for that blessed fulfillment and give habitually as if we really believed the words, *All Israel shall be saved.*

Chapter 8

The Heirs of God

For as many as are led by the Spirit of God, they are the sons of God. For ye have not received the spirit of bondage again to fear; but ye have received the Spirit of adoption, whereby we cry, Abba, Father. The Spirit itself beareth witness with our spirit, that we are the children of God: And if children, then heirs; heirs of God, and joint-heirs with Christ; if so be that we suffer with him, that we may be also glorified together. (Romans 8:14-17)

This passage of Scripture is one that ought to cause us to examine our hearts. It summons us to consider the sincere question, Am I an heir of God? Am I an heir of glory?[49]

I am not speaking of any earthly inheritance. I am not writing of matters which only concern the rich, the great, and the noble. I am not asking whether you are an heir to money or lands. I only want you to consider seriously whether you are an heir of God and an heir of glory.

The inheritance I speak of is the only inheritance really worth having. All others are unsatisfying and disappointing. They bring with them many cares. They cannot cure an aching heart. They cannot lighten a heavy conscience. They cannot keep away family troubles. They cannot

---

49 A large part of this sermon is not of a prophetic character, but I feel that it forms a fitting conclusion to the whole volume and therefore insert it unabridged.

prevent sicknesses, bereavements, separations, and deaths. But there is no disappointment among the heirs of glory.

The inheritance I speak of is the only inheritance which can be kept forever. All others must be left in the hour of death if they have not been taken away before. The owners of millions of pounds or millions of dollars can carry nothing with them beyond the grave. But it is not so with the heirs of glory. Their inheritance is eternal.

The inheritance I speak of is the only inheritance which is within everybody's reach. Most will never obtain riches and greatness though they labor hard for them all their lives. But glory, honor, and eternal life are offered to every person freely, to every person who is willing to accept them on God's terms. *Whosoever will* may be an heir of glory.

If you wish to have a portion of this inheritance, you must be a member of the one family on earth to which it belongs, and that is the family of all true Christians. You must become one of God's children on earth if you desire to have glory in heaven. If you are not one already, I write to persuade you to become a child of God today. If presently you have only a vague hope and nothing more, I write to persuade you to make sure that you are. Only true Christians are the children of God. Only the children of God are heirs of glory. Give me your attention as I try to explain these things to you and show you the lessons which the verses of our text contain.

1. What is the relationship of all true Christians to God?

2. What are the special evidences of this relationship?

3. What are the special privileges of this relationship?

First let me show you that the relationship of all true Christians to God is that of sons. They are God's *sons*. I know no higher and more comfortable word that could have been chosen. To be servants of God, to be subjects, soldiers, disciples, and friends – all of these are excellent titles. But to be the *sons* of God is a step higher still. What does the Scripture say? *The servant abideth not in the house for ever: but the Son abideth ever* (John 8:35).

To be a son of the rich and noble in this world, to be a son of the princes and kings of the earth – this is counted a privilege. But to be a son of the King of Kings and Lord of Lords, to be a son of the High and Holy One who inhabits eternity – this is something higher still. And yet this is the share of every true Christian.

The son of an earthly parent naturally looks to his father for affection, provision, and education. There is a home always open to him. There is a love which no bad conduct can completely extinguish. All these are things that belong even to the sons of this world. Think then how great is the privilege of that poor sinner of mankind who can say of God, "He is my Father."

But how can sinful people like you and I become sons of God? When do we enter into this glorious relationship? We are not the sons of God by nature. We are not born that way when we come into the world. No person has a natural right to look to God as his Father. It is a vile heresy to say that he has. Men are said to be born poets and painters, but men are never born sons of God. Ephesians tells us, *[Ye] were by nature the children of wrath, even as others* (Ephesians 2:3). John says, *The children of God are manifest, and the children of the devil: whosoever doeth not righteousness is not of God* (1 John 3:10). The catechism of the Church of England wisely follows the doctrine of the Bible and teaches us to say, "We are by nature born in sin, and children of wrath." Yes, we are born children of the devil, not children of God! Sin is indeed hereditary and runs in the family of Adam. Grace is anything but hereditary, and holy men do not have, as a matter of course, holy sons. How, then, and when does this mighty change come upon men? When and in what manner do sinners become the sons and daughters of the Lord Almighty?

> We are not the sons of God by nature.

People become sons of God in the day that the Spirit leads them to believe on Jesus Christ for salvation and not before.[50] What does Galatians say? *Ye are all the children of God by faith in Christ Jesus* (Galatians 3:26). What does the epistle to the Corinthians say? *Of him are ye in Christ Jesus* (1 Corinthians 1:30). What does the Gospel of John say? *As many as received him, to them gave he power* [or privilege] *to become the sons of God, even to them that believe on his name* (John 1:12). Faith unites

---

50   The reader will of course understand that I am not speaking now of children who die in infancy, or of persons who live and die mentally unable to believe.

sinners to the Son of God and makes them one of His members. Faith makes them one of those in whom the Father sees no spot and is well pleased. Faith marries them to the beloved Son of God and entitles them to be counted among the sons. Faith gives them fellowship with the Father and the Son. Faith grafts them into the Father's family and opens up to them a room in the Father's house. Faith gives them life instead of death and makes them sons instead of servants. Show me those that have this faith, and whatever be their church or denomination, I say that they are sons of God.

This is one of those points you should never forget. You and I know nothing of a person's sonship until they believe. No doubt the sons of God are foreknown and chosen from all eternity and predestinated to adoption. But remember, it is not until they are called in due time and believe – it is not until then that you and I can be certain they are sons. It is not until they repent and believe that the angels of God rejoice over them. The angels cannot read the book of God's election; they do not know who His hidden ones are in the earth. They rejoice over no one until they believe. But when they see sinners repenting and believing, then there is joy among them – joy that one more stick is plucked from the fire and one more son and heir is born again to the Father in heaven. But once more I say, you and I know nothing certain about people's sonship to God until they believe in Christ.

I warn everyone to beware of the deceptive notion that all men and women are children of God whether they have faith in Christ or not. It is a wild theory which many are clinging to today but one which cannot be proved out of the Word of God. It is a dangerous dream with which many are trying to soothe themselves, but one from which there will be a fearful waking-up at the last day.

I do not pretend to deny that in a certain sense God is the universal Father of all mankind. He is the Great First Cause of all things. He is the Creator of all mankind, and in Him alone, all people, whether Christians or heathens, live and move and have their being (Acts 17:28). All this is unquestionably true. In this sense Paul told the Athenians that a poet of their own had said, *We are also his offspring* (Acts 17:28). But this sonship does not give a person a title to heaven. The sonship which we have by creation is the same one that belongs to stones, trees, beasts, and even to the devils.

I do not deny that God loves all mankind with a love of pity and compassion. *His tender mercies are over all his works* (Psalm 145:9). He is *not willing that any should perish, but that all should come to repentance* (2 Peter 3:9). He has *no pleasure in the death of him that dieth* (Ezekiel 18:32). I admit all this fully. In this sense our Lord Jesus tells us, *God so loved the world, that he gave his only begotten Son, that whosoever believeth in him should not perish, but have everlasting life* (John 3:16).

But God is a reconciled and pardoning Father only to those who are members of His Son Jesus Christ, and members are those who believe on Jesus Christ for salvation. Anything else I utterly deny. The holiness and justice of God are both against the doctrine of universalism – the false teaching that all people are the sons of God. God's holiness and justice make it impossible for sinful men to approach God except through a mediator. They tell us that God out of Christ is a consuming fire. The whole system of the New Testament is against the doctrine. The New Testament teaches that no man can claim an interest in Christ unless he will receive Him as his Mediator and believe on Him as his Savior. Where there is no faith in Christ, it is absurd folly to say that someone may take comfort in God as his Father. God is a reconciled Father to none but the members of Christ!

It is nonsense to talk of the view I am now endorsing as narrow-minded and harsh. The gospel sets an open door before every person. Its promises are wide and full. Its invitations are earnest and tender. Its requirements are simple and clear. Only believe on the Lord Jesus Christ, and, whosoever you are, you will be saved (Acts 16:31). But to say that proud people, who will not bow their necks to the easy yoke of Christ, and worldly people, who are determined to have their own way and their sins – to say that such people have a right to claim an interest in Christ and a right to call themselves sons of God is absurdity indeed. God offers to be their Father, but He does it on certain distinct terms: they must approach Him through Christ. Christ offers to be their Savior, but in doing it He makes one simple requirement: they must commit their souls to Him and give Him their hearts. They refuse the terms, and yet dare to call God their Father! They scorn the requirement, but dare to hope that Christ will save them! They want God to be their Father, but on their own terms! They want Christ to be their Savior, but on their own conditions! What can be more unreasonable? What can be more proud? What can be more unholy than such a doctrine as this? Be careful, for it is a common doctrine in these latter days. Watch out for it, for it is often beguilingly put forward and sounds beautiful and charitable in the mouths of poets, novelists, sentimentalists, and tenderhearted women. Beware of it unless you mean to throw aside your Bible altogether and set yourself up to be wiser than God. Stand firm on the old scriptural ground – No sonship to God without Christ! No part in Christ without faith!

I wish there was not so much cause for giving warnings of this kind, but I have reason to think they need to be given clearly and unmistakably. There is a school of theology growing today that appears to me most uniquely calculated to promote unbelief, to help the devil, and to ruin souls. It comes to us, like Joab to Amasa (2 Samuel 20), with the highest professions of charity, liberality, and love. According to this theology, God is all mercy and love. His holiness and justice are completely left out of sight! Hell is never spoken of in this theology; its talk is all of heaven! Damnation is never mentioned; it is treated as an impossible thing. "All men and women are to be saved! Faith and the work of the Spirit are refined away into nothing at all! Everybody who believes anything has faith! Everybody who thinks anything has the Spirit! Everybody is right! Nobody is wrong! No one is to blame for any actions they may commit! It is the result of their station in life! It is the effect of circumstances! They are not accountable for their opinions any more than for the color of their skin! People must be allowed to be what they are! The Bible, of course, is a very imperfect book! It is old-fashioned! It is obsolete! We may believe just as much of it as we please and no more!"

I warn you solemnly to beware and stay away from all this theology. In spite of big, lofty words about "liberality," "charity," "broad views," "new lights," "freedom from bigotry," and so forth, I do believe it to be a theology that leads to hell rather than to heaven.

Facts, also, are directly against the teachers of this theology. Let them walk around the wards of hospitals and note the many diseases that afflict our bodies. Let them go to the shores of the Dead Sea and look down into its mysterious, bitter waters. Let them observe the wandering Jews scattered over the face of the world. And then let them tell us, if they dare, that God is so entirely a God of mercy and love that He never does and never will punish sin.

The conscience of man is directly against these teachers. Let them go to the bedside of some dying child and try to comfort him with their doctrines. Let them see if their celebrated theories will calm his gnawing, restless anxiety about the future and enable him to depart in peace. Let them show us, if they can, a few well-authenticated cases of joy and happiness in death without Bible promises, without conversion, and without the faith in the blood of Christ that is taught by old-fashioned theology. When people are leaving this world, conscience makes sad work of these new belief systems. In a dying hour, our consciences are not easily satisfied that there is no such thing as hell.

Every reasonable conception that we can form of a future state is directly against these teachers. Imagine a heaven which contains all mankind! Fancy a heaven in which holy and unholy, pure and impure, good and bad are all gathered together in one confused mass! What point of union would there be in such a company? What common bond of harmony and brotherhood? What common delight in a common service? What state of agreement, what harmony, what peace, what oneness of spirit could exist? Certainly our minds are revolted by the idea of a heaven in which there is no distinction between the righteous and the wicked, between Pharaoh and Moses, between Abraham and the Sodomites, between Paul and Nero, between Peter and Judas Iscariot, between the man who dies in the act of murder or drunkenness and men like Baxter, Wilberforce, and M'Cheyne![51] Surely an eternity in such a miserably confused crowd would be worse than annihilation itself! Such a heaven would be no better than hell!

The interests of all holiness and morality are directly against these teachers. If all men and women alike are God's children, what is the

---

51 This refers to Richard Baxter, an English poet and theologian; William Wilberforce, a British politician and instigator of the end of the slave trade; and Robert Murray M'Cheyne, a Scottish pastor and poet remembered now for his Bible-reading plan.

difference between them in how they live their lives? And if all are going to heaven, however different they may be from one another here in the world, what is the use of laboring after holiness at all? What motive remains for living *soberly, righteously, and godly* (Titus 2:12)? What does it matter how we conduct ourselves if we all go to heaven and nobody goes to hell? Surely the very heathen of Greece and Rome could tell us something better and wiser than this! Undeniably, a doctrine which is subversive of holiness and morality and takes away all motives for effort carries on the face of it the stamp of its origin. It is of earth, not of heaven. It is of the devil, not of God.

The Bible is against these teachers from beginning to end. Hundreds of texts might be quoted which are diametrically opposed to their theories. If the Bible is to square with their views, these texts must be instantly rejected. There may be no valid reason why they should be rejected, but to suit their theology they must be thrown away. At this rate, the authority of the whole Bible will soon come to an end. But what do they give us in place of God's Word that they have taken out of our hands? Nothing, nothing at all! They rob us of the Bread of Life and do not give us so much as a stone in its place.

Once more I warn you to be on your guard against this theology. I charge you to hold fast the doctrine which I have been trying hard to uphold in this address. Remember what I have said and never let it go. No inheritance of glory without sonship to God! No sonship to God without an interest or share in Christ! No interest in Christ without your own personal faith! This is God's truth. Never renounce it.

Do you want to know if you are a son of God? Ask yourself this day, and ask it as if you are in God's sight, if you have repented and believed. Ask yourself if you are by experience acquainted with Christ and united to Him in heart. If not, you may be sure you are no son of God. You are not yet born again. You are still in your sins. God may be your Father through creation, but He is not your reconciled and pardoning Father. Even though church and world agree to tell you to the contrary, and clergy and laity unite in flattering you – your sonship is worth little or nothing in the sight of God. *Let God be true, but every man a liar.* Without faith in Christ, you are no son of God – you are not born again.

Do you desire to become a son of God? If you see your sins and flee to Christ for salvation, this day you will be placed among the children. Acknowledge your iniquity and grab hold of the hand that Jesus holds out to you this day, and sonship, with all its privileges, is your own. Confess your sins and bring them to Christ, and God *is faithful and just to forgive us our sins, and to cleanse us from all unrighteousness* (1 John 1:9). This very day, old things will pass away, and all things become new. This very day you will be forgiven, pardoned, and accepted in the beloved. Today you will have a new name given to you in heaven. You started out reading this as a child of wrath, but tonight you will lie down as a child of God. If your professed desire of sonship is sincere, if you are truly weary of your sins and have something more than a lazy wish to be free, then there is real comfort for you. It is all true. It is all written in Scripture, even as I have put it down. I dare not raise barriers between you and God. This day I say, "Believe on the Lord Jesus Christ, and you will be a son and be saved."

Are you already a son of God? Rejoice and be exceedingly glad of your privileges! Rejoice, for you have good reason to be thankful. Remember the words of the beloved apostle: *Behold, what manner of love the Father hath bestowed upon us, that we should be called the sons of God* (1 John 3:1). How wonderful that heaven should look down on earth, that the Holy God should set His mind on sinful man and admit him into His family! What does it matter if the world does not understand you? What if the men of this world laugh at you and cast out your name as evil? Let them laugh. God is your Father. You have no need to be ashamed. The queen can create a nobleman. The bishops can ordain clergymen. But queens, lords, and commons, bishops, priests, and deacons – all together cannot, of their own power, make one son of God, or one of greater dignity than a son of God. People who can call God their Father and Christ their older Brother – those people may be poor and lowly, but they never need to be ashamed.

Let me show you, now, the special evidences of the true Christian's relationship to God. How can you make sure of your own sonship? How will you find out if you are one who has come to Christ by faith and been born again? What are the marks, signs, and tokens by which the sons of God can be known? This is a question that all who love eternal life need to ask. The verses of Scripture I am asking you to consider, as well as many others, supply the answer. True Christians are led by the Spirit, they have the Spirit of adoption, they have the witness of the Spirit, and they suffer with Christ.

The sons of God are all led by His Spirit. What does Scripture say? *As many as are led by the Spirit of God, they are the sons of God* (Romans 8:14). They are all under the leading and teaching of the unseen, almighty power of the Holy Spirit. The sons of God no longer turn to their own ways, walk in the light of their own eyes, or follow their own natural heart's desires. The Spirit leads them. The Spirit guides them. There is a movement in their hearts, lives, and affections which they feel, though they may not be able to explain, and a movement which is always more or less in the same direction.

They are led away from sin, away from self-righteousness, away from the world. This is the road by which the Spirit leads God's children.

Those whom God adopts He teaches and trains. He shows them their own hearts. He makes them weary of their own ways. He makes them long for inward peace.

They are led to Christ. They are led to the Bible. They are led to prayer. They are led to holiness. This is the beaten path along which the Spirit makes them travel. Those whom God adopts He always sanctifies. He makes sin very bitter to them and He makes holiness very sweet.

It is the Spirit who leads them to Sinai and shows them the law so that their hearts may be broken. It is He who leads them to Calvary and shows them the cross so that their hearts may be bandaged and healed. It is He who leads them to Pisgah and gives them distant views of the promised land so that their hearts may be cheered. When they are taken into the wilderness and taught to see their own emptiness, it is by the leading of the Spirit. When they are carried up to Tabor and lifted up with glimpses of the glory to come, it is by the leading of the Spirit. Each and all of God's sons are the subject of these leadings. Each and all yield themselves willingly to them. And each and all are led by the right way to a city where they can live.

Put this deep in your heart, and do not let it go. The sons of God are a people led by the Spirit of God and always led more or less in the same way. Their experience will correspond wonderfully when they compare notes in heaven. This is one mark of sonship.

Furthermore, **all the sons of God have the feelings of adopted children** towards their Father in heaven. What does the Scripture say? *Ye have not received the spirit of bondage again to fear; but ye have received the Spirit of adoption, whereby we cry, Abba, Father* (Romans 8:15).

The sons of God are delivered from that oppressive fear of God that sin creates in the natural heart. They are redeemed from that feeling of guilt that made Adam hide himself in the trees of the garden and Cain go out from the presence of the Lord. They are no longer afraid of God's holiness and justice and majesty. They no longer feel as if there were a great gulf and barrier between themselves and God, and as if God were angry with them and must be angry with them because of their sins. The sons of God are delivered from these chains and fetters of the soul.

Their feelings towards God are now those of peace and confidence. They see Him as a Father reconciled in Christ Jesus. They look on Him as a God whose attributes are all satisfied by their great Mediator and Peacemaker, the Lord Jesus, and as a God who is just and yet the Justifier of everyone who believes on Jesus. As their Father, the sons can draw near to Him with boldness. As their Father, they can speak to Him with freedom. They have exchanged the spirit of bondage for that of liberty and the spirit of fear for that of love. They know that God is holy, but they are not afraid. They know that they are sinners, but they are not frightened. Though God is holy, they believe that He is completely reconciled. Though they are sinners, they believe they are clothed all over with Jesus Christ. That is how the sons of God feel.

I admit that some of them feel this more vividly than others. Some of them carry around with them scraps and remnants of the old spirit of bondage to their dying day. Many of them have fits and spasms of the old man's complaint of fear return to them at intervals. But very few of the sons of God could be found who would not say, if cross-examined, that since they have known Christ they have had very different feelings towards God than they ever had before. They feel as if something like the old Roman form of adoption had taken place between themselves and their Father in heaven. They feel as if He had said to each one of them, "Will you be my son?" and as if their hearts had replied, "I will."

Try to grasp and hold this also: the sons of God are people who feel towards God in a way that the children of the world do not. They feel no more oppressive fear towards Him. They feel toward Him as a reconciled parent. This is another mark of sonship.

The sons of God have **the witness of the Spirit** in their consciences. What does the Scripture say? *The Spirit itself beareth witness with our spirit, that we are the children of God* (Romans 8:16).

They have all got something within their hearts which tells them there is a relationship between themselves and God. They feel something which tells them that old things are passed away and all things have become new. It tells them that guilt is gone, peace is restored, heaven's door is open, and hell's door is shut. They have what the children of the world do not have – a felt, positive, reasonable hope. They have what Paul calls the *seal* (Ephesians 1:13) and *earnest* (2 Corinthians 1:22) of the Spirit.

I do not deny that this witness of the Spirit varies greatly in the extent that the sons of God possess it. With some it is a loud, clear, ringing, and distinct testimony of conscience: "I am Christ's, and Christ is mine." With others it is a little, feeble, stammering whisper that the devil and the flesh often prevent from being heard. Some of the children of God speed on their course toward heaven under the full sails of assurance. Others are tossed to and fro all their voyage and will scarcely believe they have faith. But take the least and lowest of the sons of God. Ask him if he will give up the little bit of religious hope that he has attained. Ask him if he will exchange his heart, with all its doubts and conflicts, its struggles and fears – ask him if he will exchange that heart for the heart of the utterly worldly and careless man. Ask him if he would be content to turn around and throw down the things he is holding and go back to the world. Who can doubt his answer? "I cannot do that," he would reply. "I do not know if I have faith, and I do not feel sure that I have grace, but I do have something within me that I do not want to part with." And what is that *something*? I will tell you. It is the witness of the Spirit.

Try to understand this: the sons of God have the witness of the Spirit in their consciences, which is another mark of sonship.

One thing more. All the sons of God **take part in suffering with Christ.** What does the Scripture say? *If children, then heirs; heirs of God, and joint-heirs with Christ; if so be that we suffer with him* (Romans 8:17).

All the children of God have a cross to carry. They have trials, troubles, and afflictions to go through for the gospel's sake. They have trials from the world, trials from the flesh, and trials from the devil. They have trials of feeling rejection from relatives and friends – hard words, hard conduct, and hard judgment. They have trials in the matter of character – slander, misrepresentation, mockery, insinuation of false motives. All of these often rain thick upon them. They have trials in the matter of the affairs of this world. They often have to choose whether they will please man and lose glory or gain glory and offend man. They have trials from their own hearts. They each have their own thorn in the flesh. This is the experience of the sons of God.

Some of them suffer more and some less. Some of them suffer in one way and some in another. God measures out their portions like a wise physician, and He cannot err. But I do not believe there was ever one child of God who reached paradise without a cross.

Suffering is the diet of the Lord's family. *Whom the Lord loveth he chasteneth* (Hebrews 12:6). *If ye be without chastisement, . . . then are ye bastards, and not sons* (Hebrews 12:8). *We must through much tribulation enter into the kingdom of God* (Acts 14:22). When Bishop Latimer[52] was told by his landlord that he had never had a trouble, "then," said he, "God cannot be here."

Suffering is a part of the process by which the sons of God are sanctified. They are chastened to wean them from the world and to make them partakers of God's holiness. The Captain of their salvation was made perfect through sufferings, and so are they. There has never been a great saint who did not have either great afflictions or great corruptions. I agree with Philip Melanchthon who said, "Where there are no cares, there will generally be no prayers."

Try to hold this in your heart also. All the sons of God have to bear a

---

52   Hugh Latimer was an Anglican preacher, chaplain, and eventually, a martyr.

cross. A suffering Savior usually has suffering disciples. The Bridegroom of the church was *a man of sorrows* (Isaiah 53:3). The bride must not be a woman of pleasures and unacquainted with grief. Blessed are they that mourn! Let us not complain of the cross. This also is a sign of sonship. No cross, no crown!

Do not suppose that you are a son of God unless you have the scriptural marks of sonship. Take care to avoid a sonship without evidence. When a person has no leading of the Spirit to show me, no spirit of adoption to tell of, no witness of the Spirit in his conscience, no cross in his experience – is this man a son of God? God forbid that I should say so! He is not marked with the mark of God's children. He is no heir of glory.

Do not tell me that you have been baptized and taught the catechism of the Church of England and therefore must be a child of God. I tell you that the infant baptism register is not the Book of Life. I tell you that to be christened a child of God and called regenerate in infancy by the faith and charity of the prayer book is one thing, but to be a child of God in truth is another thing altogether. Go read that catechism again. It is the "death unto sin and the new birth unto righteousness" that makes men children of grace. Unless you know these by experience, you are no son of God.

Do not tell me that you are a member of Christ's church and so must be a son. I answer that the sons of the church are not necessarily the sons of God. Such sonship is not the sonship of the eighth chapter of Romans. If you are to be saved, that is the sonship you must have.

And now some of you will want to know if you may be saved without the witness of the Spirit. I answer that if you mean without the full assurance of hope, you may be saved without question. But if you want to know if you can be saved without any inward sense, or knowledge, or hope of salvation, I answer that ordinarily you cannot. I warn you plainly to get rid of all indecision about your state before God and to make your calling sure. Clear up your position and relationship. Do not think there is anything praiseworthy in always doubting. Leave that to the Roman Catholic. Do not think it is wise to always be living like the borderers of old time, on the "debatable ground."[53] "Assurance," said

---
53 When England and Scotland were two distinct countries, the "debatable ground" was

old Puritan John Dod, "may be attained: and what have we been doing all our lives since we became Christians if we have not attained it?"

I do not doubt that some of you true Christians will think your evidence of sonship is too small to be good and will write bitter things against yourselves. Let me try to cheer you. Who gave you the feelings you possess? Who made you hate sin? Who made you love Christ? Who made you long and labor to be holy? From where did these feelings come? Did they come from nature? There are no such products in a natural man's heart. Did they come from the devil? He would gladly stifle such feelings altogether. Cheer up and take courage. Do not be afraid, and do not be discouraged. Press forward and go on. There is hope for you after all. Strive. Labor. Seek. Ask. Knock. Follow on. You will see that you are sons of God.

> Cheer up and take courage. Do not be afraid, and do not be discouraged. Press forward and go on.

Last, let me show you the privileges of the true Christian's relationship to God. Nothing you can think of would be more glorious than the prospects of the sons of God. The words of Scripture which began this address contain a rich mine of good and comforting things. *If [we are] children,* says Paul, *then [we are] heirs; heirs of God, and joint-heirs with Christ; . . . that we may be also glorified together* (Romans 8:17).

True Christians, then, are heirs. Something is prepared for them all which is yet to be revealed.

They are heirs of God. To be heirs of the rich on earth is something. How much more then is it to be a son and heir of the King of Kings!

They are joint-heirs with Christ. They will share in His majesty and take part in His glory. They will be glorified together with Him.

And this, remember, is for all the children. Abraham took care to provide for all his children, and God takes care to provide for His. None of them are disinherited. None will be cast out. None will be cut off. Each will stand in his lot and have a portion in the day when the Lord brings many sons to glory.

Who can explain the full nature of the inheritance of the saints in light? Who can describe the glory which is yet to be revealed and given

---

a section of land claimed by both countries. The borderers were those who lived in this disputed area.

to the children of God? Words fail us. Language falls short. Mind cannot conceive fully and tongue cannot express perfectly the things that are contained in the glory yet to come upon the sons and daughters of the Lord Almighty. It is indeed a true saying of the apostle John: *It doth not yet appear what we shall be* (1 John 3:2).

The Bible itself only lifts a little the veil that hangs over this subject. How could it do more? We could not thoroughly understand more if we had been told more. The condition of our mind is still too earthly, and our understanding is still too worldly to appreciate more if we had it. The Bible generally deals with the subject in negative terms, not in positive assertions. It describes more of what there will not be in the glorious inheritance, and so we get some faint idea of what there will be. It paints the absence of certain things in order that we may drink in a little of the blessedness of the things present. It tells us that the inheritance is *incorruptible, and undefiled, and that fadeth not away* (1 Peter 1:4). It tells us that the crown of glory *fadeth not away* (1 Peter 5:4). It tells us that the devil is to be bound, that there shall be no more night and no more curse, that death shall be cast into the lake of fire, that all tears shall be wiped away, and that the inhabitants will no more say, "I am sick." These are glorious things! No corruption! No fading! No withering! No devil! No curse of sin! No sorrow! No tears! No sickness! No death! Surely the cup of the children of God will indeed run over!

But there are positive things we are told about the glory yet to come on the heirs of God which we should not keep back. There are many sweet, pleasant, and indescribable comforts in their future inheritance which all true Christians should consider. There are refreshments for fainting pilgrims in many of the words and expressions of Scripture that you and I ought to store up for a time of need.

Is **knowledge** pleasant to us now? Is the little that we know of God, Christ, and the Bible precious to our souls, and do we long for more? We will have it perfectly in glory. What does the Scripture say? *Then shall I know even as also I am known* (1 Corinthians 13:12). Blessed be God, in heaven there will be no more disagreements among believers! Episcopalians and Presbyterians, Calvinists and Arminians, Millenarians and Amillenarians, friends of establishment churches and friends of the voluntary church system, advocates of infant baptism and advocates of adult baptism – all will at length see eye to eye. The former ignorance will have passed away. We will marvel to find how childish and blind we have been.

Is **holiness** pleasant to us now? Is sin the burden and bitterness of our lives? Do we long for entire conformity to the image of God? We will have it perfectly in glory. What does the Scripture say? Christ gave Himself for the church, *that he might present it to himself a glorious church, not having spot, or wrinkle, or any such thing* (Ephesians 5:27). Oh, the blessedness of an eternal goodbye to sin! How little even the best of us do now! What awful corruption sticks like glue to all our motives, all our thoughts, all our words, and all our actions! So many of us, like Naphtali, are excellent in our words, but like Reuben, are unstable in our works! Thank God, all this will be changed!

Is **rest** pleasant to us now? Do we often feel faint while we are striving? Do we long for a world in which we need not be always watching and warring? We shall have it perfectly in glory. What does the Scripture say? *There remaineth therefore a rest to the people of God* (Hebrews 4:9). The daily, hourly conflict with the world, the flesh, and the devil will at last be at an end. The Enemy will be bound. The warfare will be over. The wicked will at last stop troubling and afflicting. The weary will at last be at rest. There will be a great calm.

Is **service** pleasant to us now? Do we find it sweet to work for Christ, and yet groan, being burdened by a feeble body? Is our spirit often willing but hampered and obstructed by the poor, weak flesh? Have our hearts burned within us when we have been allowed to give a cup of cold water for Christ's sake, but have we sighed when we think what unprofitable servants we are? Be encouraged to know we will be able to serve perfectly and without weariness in glory. What does the Scripture say? *[They] serve him day and night in his temple* (Revelation 7:15).

Is **satisfaction** pleasant to us now? Do we find the world empty? Do we long for the filling up of every void place and gap in our hearts? We will have it perfectly in glory. We will no longer have to mourn over cracks in all our earthen vessels, thorns on all our roses, and bitter dregs in all our sweet cups. We will no longer lament with Jonah over withered plants. We will no longer say with Solomon, *All is vanity and vexation of spirit* (Ecclesiastes 1:14). We will no longer cry with aged David, *I have seen an end of all perfection* (Psalm 119:96). What do the Scriptures say? *I shall be satisfied, when I awake, with thy likeness* (Psalm 17:15).

Is **communion with the saints** pleasant to us now? Do we feel that we are most happy when we are with the excellent of the earth? Are we never so much at home as in their company? We will have it perfectly in glory. What does the Scripture say? *The Son of man shall send forth his angels, and they shall gather out of his kingdom all things that offend, and them which do iniquity* (Matthew 13:41). *He shall send his angels with a great sound of a trumpet, and they shall gather together his elect from the four winds* (Matthew 24:31). Praise God! We will see all the saints of whom we have read in the Bible and in whose steps we have tried to walk. We will see apostles, prophets, patriarchs, martyrs, reformers, missionaries, and ministers of whom the world was not worthy. We will see the faces of those we have known and loved in Christ on earth and over whose departure we shed bitter tears. We will see them brighter and more glorious than they ever were before. And best of all, we will see them without hurry and anxiety and without feeling that we only meet to part again. In glory there is no death, no parting, no farewell!

Is **communion with Christ** pleasant to us now? Do we find His name precious to us? Do we feel our hearts burn within us at the thought of His dying love? We will have perfect communion with Him in glory. *So shall we ever be with the Lord* (1 Thessalonians 4:17). We will be with Him in paradise. We will see His face in the kingdom. These eyes of ours will behold those hands and feet that were pierced with nails and that head that was crowned with thorns. Where He is, there will the sons of God be. When He comes, they will come with Him. When He sits down in His glory, they will sit down by His side. What a blessed promise! I am a dying man in a dying world! All before me is dark! We do not know what the world to come is like; it is a harbor unknown! But

Christ is there, and that is enough. Surely if there is rest and peace in following Him by faith on earth, there will be far more rest and peace when we see Him face-to-face. If we have found it good to follow the pillar of cloud and fire in the wilderness, we will find it a thousand times better to sit down in our eternal inheritance with our Joshua in the promised land.

If you are not yet among the sons and heirs, I do pity you with all my heart. How much you are missing! How little true comfort you are enjoying! There you are struggling on and toiling in the fire and wearying yourself for mere earthly ends. You seek rest and find none, chase shadows and never catch them, wonder why you are not happy but refuse to see the cause; you are hungry, thirsty, empty, and blind to the plenty within your reach. Oh, I wish you were wise, that you would hear the voice of Jesus and learn of Him!

If you are one of those who are sons and heirs, you can rejoice and be happy. You can wait contentedly like the boy Patience in *Pilgrim's Progress*. Your best things are yet to come. You can bear crosses without complaint. Your light affliction is but for a moment. *The sufferings of this present time are not worthy to be compared with the glory which shall be revealed* (Romans 8:18). *When Christ, who is our life, shall appear, then shall ye also appear with him in glory* (Colossians 3:4). You need not envy the transgressor and his prosperity. You are the truly rich. A dying believer in my own parish said, "I am more rich than I ever was in my life." You may say as Mephibosheth said to David, "Let the world take all; my King is coming again in peace." You may say as Alexander said when he gave all his riches away and was asked what he kept for himself: "I have hope." You do not need to be discouraged by sickness; the eternal part of you is safe and provided for, whatever happens to your body. You can look calmly on death; it opens a door between you and your inheritance. You do not need to sorrow excessively over the things of the world – over partings and bereavements, losses and crosses. The day of gathering is coming. Your treasure is out of harm's reach. Every year heaven becomes fuller with those you love and earth emptier. Glory in your inheritance! It is all yours if you are a son of God. If we are children, then we are heirs.

> If we are children, then we are heirs.

And now in conclusion, let me ask you, Whose child are you? Are you the child of nature or the child of grace? Are you the child of the devil or the child of God? You cannot be both at the same time. Which are you?

Work out the answer because you will die as one or the other. It can be settled, so it is foolish to leave it in doubt. Resolve it because time is short, the world is getting old, and you are fast drawing near to the judgment seat of Christ. Settle it, for death is near, the Lord is at hand, and who can tell what a day might bring? Oh, do not rest until the question is settled! Never feel satisfied until you can say, "I have been born again; I am a son of God."

If you are not a son and an heir of God, let me beg you to become one without delay. Do you want to be rich? There are unsearchable riches in Christ. Do you desire to be noble? If you believe in Christ, you will be a king. Do you want to be happy? You will have a peace that passes understanding and that the world can never give nor take away. Come out, take up the cross, and follow Christ! Come out from among the thoughtless and the worldly and hear the word of the Lord: *I will receive you. And will be a Father unto you, and ye shall be my sons and daughters, saith the Lord Almighty* (2 Corinthians 6:17-18).

If you are a son of God, I call on you to walk worthy of your Father's house. I charge you sincerely to honor Him in your life, and above all, to honor Him by complete obedience to all His commands and a hearty love for all His children. Labor to travel through the world like a child of God and an heir of glory. Let men be able to trace a family likeness between you and your Father. Live a heavenly life. Seek things that are above. Do not appear to be building your nest below. Behave like someone who is looking for a city out of sight, whose citizenship is in heaven, and who is willing to put up with many hardships until he gets home.

Labor to feel like a son of God in every situation in which you are placed. Never forget you are on your Father's ground as long as you are here on earth. Never forget that a Father's hand sends all your mercies and your crosses. Cast every care on Him. Be happy and cheerful in Him. Why should you ever be sad if you are the King's son? People should not wonder when they look at you if it is a good thing to be one of God's children.

Strive to behave toward others like a son of God. Be gentle and blameless in your day and generation. Be a peacemaker among all you know. Seek for your children sonship to God above everything else. Whatever else you do for them, seek for them an inheritance in heaven. No parents leave their children so well provided for as those who leave them as sons and heirs of God.

If you are a son of God, persevere in your Christian calling, and keep moving forward. Be careful to lay aside every weight and the sin that most easily trips you up. Keep your eyes steadily fixed on Jesus. Abide in Him. Remember that without Him you can do nothing and with Him you can do all things (John 15:5; Philippians 4:13). Watch and pray daily. *Be ye stedfast, unmoveable, always abounding in the work of the Lord* (1 Corinthians 15:58). Make it clear in your heart that not a cup of cold water given in the name of a disciple will lose its reward, and that every year you are so much nearer to home.

In just a little while He who is coming will come and will not tarry. Then will be the glorious liberty and the full display of the sons of God. Then will the world acknowledge that they were the truly wise. The sons of God will at last come of age, and they will no longer be heirs of expectancy but heirs in possession. And then they will hear with exceeding joy those comfortable words: *Come, ye blessed of my Father, inherit the kingdom prepared for you from the foundation of the world* (Matthew 25:34). Surely that day will make amends for all!

It is my heart's desire and prayer that all of you will see the value of the inheritance of glory and to one day possess it.

He which testifieth these things saith, Surely I come quickly. Amen. Even so, come, Lord Jesus. (Revelation 22:20)

"The Church Has Waited Long"

The church has waited long
Her absent Lord to see;
And still in loneliness she waits,
A friendless stranger she.

Age after age has gone,
Sun after sun has set,
And still in weeds of widowhood
She weeps, a mourner yet.

Saint after saint on earth
Has lived and loved and died;
And as they left us, one by one,
We laid them side by side.

We laid them down to sleep,
But not in hope forlorn;
We laid them but to ripen there,
Till the last glorious morn.

The serpent's brood increase,
The powers of hell grow bold,
The conflict thickens, faith is low,
And love is waxing cold.

How long, O Lord our God,
Holy and true and good,
Wilt Thou not judge Thy suffering church,
Her sighs and tears and blood?

We long to hear Thy voice,
To see Thee face-to-face,
To share Thy crown and glory then,
As now we share Thy grace.

Should not the loving bride
The absent Bridegroom mourn?
Should she not wear the weeds of grief
Until her Lord return?

The whole creation groans,
And waits to hear that voice
That shall restore her comeliness,
And make her wastes rejoice.

Come, Lord, and wipe away
The curse, the sin, the stain,
And make this blighted world of ours
Thine own fair world again.
Come, then, Lord Jesus, come!
— Horatius Bonar

J. C. Ryle – A Brief Biography

John Charles Ryle was born into a wealthy, affluent, socially elite family on May 10, 1816 – the firstborn son of John Ryle, a banker, and his wife Susanna (Wirksworth) Ryle. As the firstborn, John lived a privileged life and was set to inherit all of his father's estate and pursue a career in Parliament. His future promised to be planned and comfortable with no material needs.

J. C. Ryle attended a private school and then earned academic scholarships to Eton (1828) and the University of Oxford (1834), but he excelled in sports. He particularly made his mark in rowing and cricket. Though his pursuit of sports was short lived, he claimed that they gave him leadership gifts. "It gave me a power of commanding, managing, organizing and directing, seeing through men's capabilities and using every man in the post to which he was best suited, bearing and forbearing, keeping men around me in good temper, which I have found of infinite use on lots of occasions in life, though in very different matters."

In 1837, before graduation, Ryle contracted a serious chest infection, which caused him to turn to the Bible and prayer for the first time in over fourteen years. One Sunday he entered church late as Ephesians 2:8 was being read – slowly, phrase by phrase. John felt the Lord was speaking to him personally, and he claims to have been converted at that moment through the Word without any commentary or sermon.

His biographer wrote, "He came under conviction, was converted, and from that moment to the last recorded syllable of this life, no doubt ever lingered in John's mind that the Word of God was living and powerful, sharper than any two-edged sword."

After graduation from Oxford, John went to London to study law for his career in politics, but in 1841, his father's bank crashed. That was the end of the career in politics, for he had no funding to continue.

In later years, John wrote, "We got up one summer's morning with all the world before us as usual, and went to bed that same night completely and entirely ruined. The immediate consequences were bitter and painful in the extreme, and humiliating to the utmost degree."

And at another time, he said, "The plain fact was there was no one of the family whom it touched more than it did me. My father and mother were no longer young and in the downhill of life; my brothers and sisters, of course, never expected to live at Henbury (the family home) and naturally never thought of it as their house after a certain time. I, on the contrary, as the eldest son, twenty-five, with all the world before me, lost everything, and saw the whole future of my life turned upside down and thrown into confusion."

After this financial ruin from abundance, Ryle was a commoner – all in a day. For the first time in his life, he needed a job. His education qualified him for the clergy, so with his Oxford degree, he was ordained and entered the ministry of the Church of England. He proceeded in a totally different direction with his first assignment in the ministry at Exbury in Hampshire, but it was a rural area riddled with disease. His recurring lung infection made a difficult couple of years until he was transferred to St. Thomas in Winchester. With his commanding presence, passionately held principles, and warm disposition, John's congregation grew so large and strong it needed different accommodations.

Ryle accepted a position at that time in Helmington, Suffolk, where he had much time to read theologians like Wesley, Bunyan, Knox, Calvin, and Luther. He was a contemporary of Charles Spurgeon, Dwight Moody, George Mueller, and Hudson Taylor. He lived in the age of Dickens, Darwin, and the American Civil War. All of these influenced Ryle's understanding and theology.

His writing career began from the tragedy of the Great Yarmouth suspension bridge. On May 9, 1845, a large crowd gathered for the official grand opening festivities, but the bridge collapsed and more than a hundred people plunged into the water and drowned. The incident shocked the whole country but it led Ryle to write his first tract. He spoke of life's uncertainties and God's sure provision of salvation through Jesus Christ. Thousands of copies were sold.

That same year, he married Matilda Plumptre, but she died after only two years, leaving him with an infant daughter. In 1850, he married Jessie Walker, but she had a lingering sickness, which caused Ryle to care for her and their growing family (three sons and another daughter) for ten years until she died. In 1861, he was transferred to Stradbroke, Suffolk, where he married Henrietta Clowes.

Stradbroke, Suffolk, was Ryle's last parish, and he gained a reputation for his straightforward preaching and evangelism. Besides his travelling and preaching, he spent time writing. He wrote more than 300 pamphlets, tracts, and books. His books include *Expository Thoughts on the Gospels* (7 Volumes, 1856-1869), *Principles for Churchmen* (1884), *Home Truths, Knots Untied, Old Paths,* and *Holiness.*

His *Christian Leaders of the Eighteenth Century* (1869) is described as having "short, pithy sentences, compelling logic and penetrating insight into spiritual power." This seems to be the case with most of his writing as he preached and wrote with five main guidelines: (1) Have a clear view of the subject, (2) Use simple words, (3) Use a simple style of composition, (4) Be direct, and (5) Use plenty of anecdotes and illustrations.

In all of his success with writing, he used the royalties to pay his father's debts. He may have felt indebted to that financial ruin, for he said, "I have not the least doubts, it was all for the best. If I had not been ruined, I should never have been a clergyman, never preached a sermon, or written a tract or book."

In spite of all of the trials that Ryle experienced – financial ruin, loss of three wives, his own poor health – he learned several life lessons. First, care and tend to your own family. Second, swim against the tide when you need to. He was evangelical before it was popular and he held to principles of Scripture: justification by faith alone, substitutionary atonement, the Trinity, and preaching. Third, model Christian attitudes toward your opponents. Fourth, learn and understand church history. Important benefits come from past generations. Fifth, serve in old age; "die in the harness." And, sixth, persevere through your trials.

These were life principles that Ryle learned as he lived his life, as he preached, as he wrote, and as he spread the gospel. He was forever a supporter of evangelism and a critic of ritualism.

J. C. Ryle was recommended by Prime Minister Benjamin Disraeli to be Bishop of Liverpool in 1880 where he then worked to build churches and mission halls to reach the whole city. He retired in 1900 at the age of 83 and died later that year. His successor described him as "a man of granite with a heart of a child."

G. C. B. Davies said "a commanding presence and fearless advocacy of his principles were combined with a kind and understanding attitude in his personal relationships."

Sources:

William P. Farley, "J. C. Ryle: A 19th-century Evangelical," *Enrichment Journal,* http://enrichmentjournal.ag.org/200604/200604_120_jcryle.cfm.

"J. C. Ryle," *The Banner of Truth, https://banneroftruth.org/us/about/banner-authors/j-c-ryle/.*

"J. C. Ryle," *Theopedia, https://www.theopedia.com/john-charles-ryle.*

David Holloway, "J. C. Ryle – The Man, The Minister and The Missionary," *Bible Bulletin Board, http://www.biblebb.com/files/ryle/j_c_ryle.htm.*

Other Similar Titles

Expository Thoughts on the Gospel of John,
by J. C. Ryle

A Commentary

In the beginning was the Word, and the Word was with God, and the Word was God. – John 1:1

Wisdom, encouragement, and exhortation is contained in these pages. Not because of the author's brilliance, but because of the words of truth contained in the gospel of John. And just as the Apostle John didn't draw any attention to himself, so also J. C. Ryle clearly and wonderfully directs his words and our thoughts towards the inspired words of scripture. If we truly love God, we will love His word; and the more study His word, the more we will love God.

Available where books are sold.

Holiness
by J. C. Ryle

A thorough study of sin, salvation by faith, and the Christian's journey of sanctification.

He who wants a correct understanding of holiness must first begin by examining the vast and solemn subject of sin. He must dig down very deep if he wants to build high. Wrong views about holiness are generally traceable to wrong views about human corruption.

Practical holiness and entire self-consecration to God are not given adequate attention by modern Christians. The unsaved sometimes rightly complain that Christians are not as kind and unselfish and good-natured as those who make no profession of faith. Far too many Christians make a verbal proclamation of faith, yet remain unchanged in heart and lifestyle. But Scripture makes it clear that holiness, in its place and proportion, is quite as important as justification. Holiness, without which no one shall see the Lord (Hebrews 12:14). It is imperative that Christians are biblically and truly holy.

The aim of this book is to instruct you, equip you, and encourage you in the pursuit of holiness.

Available where books are sold.

Christian Leaders of the Eighteenth Century,
by J. C. Ryle

The reader will soon discover that I am an enthusiastic admirer of the men whose lives and ministries I have narrated in this volume. I confess it honestly. I am a thorough admirer of them. I firmly believe that, with the exceptions of Martin Luther and his contemporaries and our own martyred Reformers, the world has not seen any such men since the days of the apostles. I believe there have not been any who have preached as much clear scriptural truth, none who have lived such lives, none who have shown such courage in Christ's service, none who have suffered as much for the truth, and none who have done as much good. If anyone can name better men, he knows more than I do.

My purpose in compiling these biographies was to present to the public the lives, characters, and work of the leading ministers whom God used to revive Christianity in England in the eighteenth century. I had long believed that these great men were not sufficiently known, and as a consequence, their value and merit had not been sufficiently recognized. I thought that the church and the world should know something more than they seem to know about such men as Whitefield, Wesley, Romaine, Rowlands, Grimshaw, Berridge, Venn, Toplady, Hervey, Walker, and Fletcher. For twenty years, I waited anxiously for some worthy account of these mighty spiritual heroes. At last I became weary of waiting, and I resolved to take the pen in my own hand and do what I could in the pages of this book.

Available where books are sold.

Repentance,
by J. C. Ryle

It is indifference that leaves people alone and allows them to go their own way. It is love, tender love, that warns them and raises the cry of alarm. The cry of "Fire! Fire!" at midnight might sometimes rudely, harshly, and unpleasantly startle a person out of his sleep, but who would complain if that cry was the means of saving his life? The words *Except you repent, you will all likewise perish* might at first seem stern and severe, but they are words of love, and they could be the means of delivering precious souls from hell.

Available where books are sold.

Heaven,
by Dwight L. Moody

The goal of this book is to whet your appetite for heaven. A careful look at Scripture reveals that heaven is what every born-again believer is longing for. Our time on earth is only in a temporary dwelling place, and heaven is the true home of all God's children. A study of heaven can change how you approach each day, and even how you view others around you. As real as this life is, we are assured that heaven is just as real. While we must not neglect our present God-given duties, we must at the same time be preparing for our future home and should even be looking forward with great anticipation to our eternal home.

Available where books are sold.

Life in Christ,
by Charles H. Spurgeon

Volumes 1-8

Men who were led by the hand or groped their way along the wall to reach Jesus were touched by his finger and went home without a guide, rejoicing that Jesus Christ had opened their eyes. Jesus is still able to perform such miracles. And, with the power of the Holy Spirit, his Word will be expounded and we'll watch for the signs to follow, expecting to see them at once. Why shouldn't those who read this be blessed with the light of heaven? This is my heart's inmost desire.

I can't put fine words together. I've never studied speech. In fact, my heart loathes the very thought of intentionally speaking with fine words when souls are in danger of eternal separation from God. No, I work to speak straight to your hearts and consciences, and if there is anyone with faith to receive, God will bless them with fresh revelation.

– Charles H. Spurgeon

Available where books are sold.

www.ingramcontent.com/pod-product-compliance
Lightning Source LLC
Chambersburg PA
CBHW070139080526
44586CB00015B/1766